# CAMBRIDGE LIBRARY COLLECTION

*Books of enduring scholarly value*

## History

The books reissued in this series include accounts of historical events and movements by eye-witnesses and contemporaries, as well as landmark studies that assembled significant source materials or developed new historiographical methods. The series includes work in social, political and military history on a wide range of periods and regions, giving modern scholars ready access to influential publications of the past.

## Campaigning Experiences in Rajpootana and Central India

The diarist Mrs Henry Duberly (1829–1902), born Frances Locke, came to public attention through her *Journal Kept During the Russian War*, an 1855 account (also reissued in this series) of her experiences accompanying her husband's regiment in the Crimea, often as the only woman present. Her descriptions of military action – including the cavalry charges at Balaklava – and the hardships and gossip of army life, made it a popular success, although a dedication to Queen Victoria was declined. This 1859 volume narrates the Hussars' subsequent posting to India during the Mutiny. Describing the practicalities and privations of a 2,028 mile march through Rajputana from Bombay, and culminating in an account of the battle of Gwalior, including the news of Rani Lakshmi Bai's suicide, it illuminates the nature of military life in this tense period of Indian history, as well as the role of women on both sides of the conflict.

T0370747

Cambridge University Press has long been a pioneer in the reissuing of out-of-print titles from its own backlist, producing digital reprints of books that are still sought after by scholars and students but could not be reprinted economically using traditional technology. The Cambridge Library Collection extends this activity to a wider range of books which are still of importance to researchers and professionals, either for the source material they contain, or as landmarks in the history of their academic discipline.

Drawing from the world-renowned collections in the Cambridge University Library, and guided by the advice of experts in each subject area, Cambridge University Press is using state-of-the-art scanning machines in its own Printing House to capture the content of each book selected for inclusion. The files are processed to give a consistently clear, crisp image, and the books finished to the high quality standard for which the Press is recognised around the world. The latest print-on-demand technology ensures that the books will remain available indefinitely, and that orders for single or multiple copies can quickly be supplied.

The Cambridge Library Collection brings back to life books of enduring scholarly value (including out-of-copyright works originally issued by other publishers) across a wide range of disciplines in the humanities and social sciences and in science and technology.

# Campaigning Experiences in Rajpootana and Central India

*During the Suppression
of the Mutiny, 1857-1858*

Frances Isabella Duberly

CAMBRIDGE
UNIVERSITY PRESS

CAMBRIDGE UNIVERSITY PRESS

Cambridge, New York, Melbourne, Madrid, Cape Town,
Singapore, São Paolo, Delhi, Tokyo, Mexico City

Published in the United States of America by Cambridge University Press, New York

www.cambridge.org
Information on this title: www.cambridge.org/9781108044752

© in this compilation Cambridge University Press 2012

This edition first published 1859
This digitally printed version 2012

ISBN 978-1-108-04475-2 Paperback

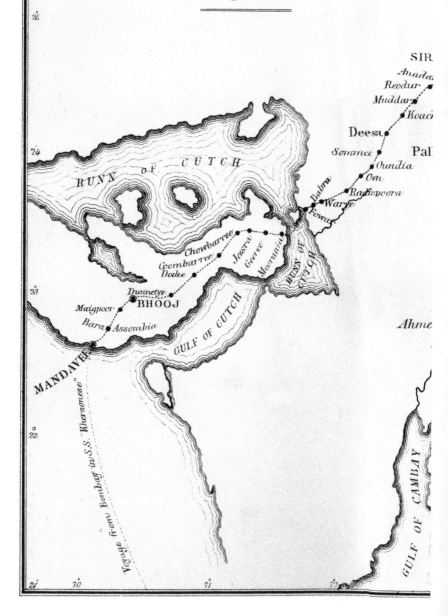

# R O U T E
### From the 31ˢᵗ January to the
### 21ˢᵗ September 1858.

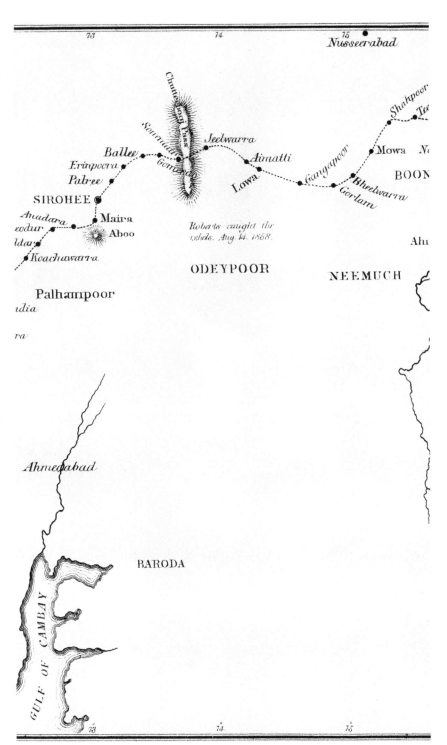

73
74
75
Nusseerabad

Chuttebooj Pass
Shahpoor
Tee

Souramun
Jeelwarra
Ballee
Mowa No
Aimatti
Gangapoor
Erinpoora
Palree
Gonzado
Lowa
Bheelwarra
BOON
SIROHEE
Gorlam

Anadara
Maira
Roberts caught the
eodur
Aboo
rebels. Aug. 14. 1858.
Ahı
Idar
Keachawarra
ODEYPOOR
NEEMUCH

Palhampoor
idia

ra

Ahmedabad

BARODA

GULF OF CAMBAY

73
74
75

Published by Smith, Elder & Cº London, 1859.

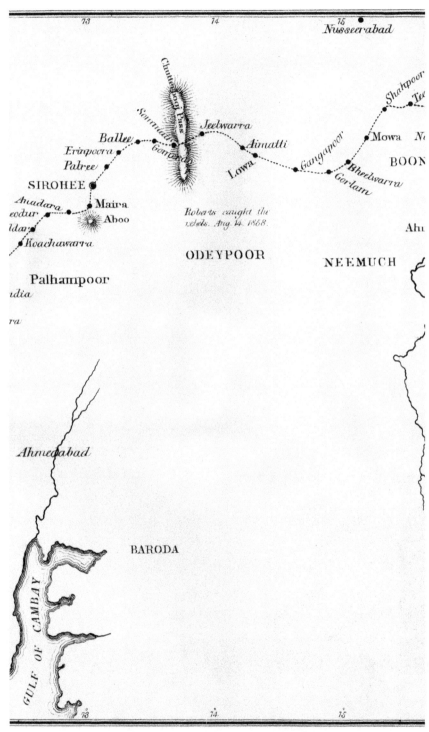

73     74     75 Nusseerabad

Chuttooj Pass

Shahpoor

Tee

Souraut

Jeelwarra

Ballee

Erinpoora

Palree

Ganora

Aimatti

Mowa

N

Lowa

Gangapoor

BOON

SIROHEE

Maira

Aboo

Anadara

eodur

lda

Koachuwarra

Gorlam

Bheelwarra

Ahu

Roberts caught the
rebels. Aug. 14. 1868.

ODEYPOOR

NEEMUCH

Palhampoor

dia

ra

Ahmedabad

BARODA

GULF OF CAMBAY

73     74     75

Published by Smith, Elder & Cº London, 1859.

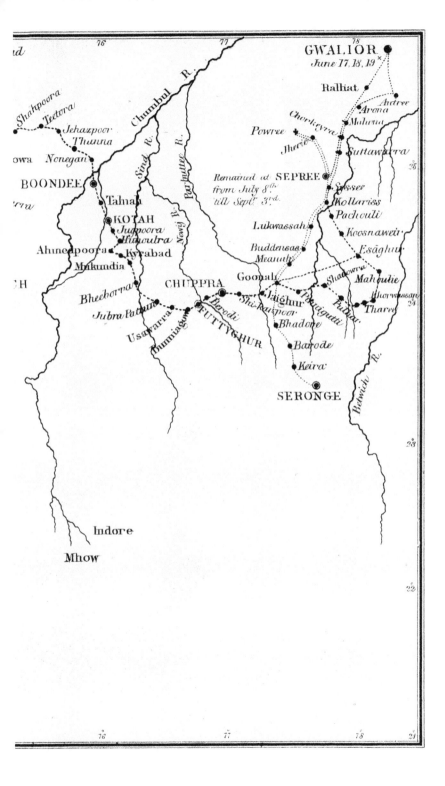

# CAMPAIGNING EXPERIENCES

IN

## RAJPOOTANA AND CENTRAL INDIA,

DURING THE

## SUPPRESSION OF THE MUTINY,

1857—1858.

BY

MRS. HENRY DUBERLY,

AUTHOR OF "A JOURNAL KEPT DURING THE RUSSIAN WAR."

" 'Tis I who here attempt unusual strains,
Of hosts unsung and unfrequented plains,
Where India reddens to the early dawn."
BEATTIE.

" In brief, a braver choice of dauntless spirits
Than now the English bottoms have waft o'er,
Did never float upon the swelling tide,
To do offence or scath to heathendom."
SHAKSPEARE.

*WITH MAPS.*

## LONDON:

PUBLISHED BY SMITH, ELDER AND CO.,
65, CORNHILL.

1859.

# Dedication.

As one who, walking in the twilight gloom,
   Hears round about him voices as it darkens,
And seeing not the forms from which they come,
   Pauses from time to time, and turns and hearkens;

So, walking here in twilight, oh! my friends,
   I hear your voices, softened by the distance,
And pause, and turn to listen as each sends
   His words of friendship, kindness, and assistance.

   *        *        *        *        *

Perhaps on earth I never shall behold
   With eye of sense your outward form and semblance:
Therefore to me ye never will grow old,
   But live for ever young in my remembrance.

Never grow old, nor change, nor pass away!
   Your gentle voices will flow on for ever,
When life grows bare and leafless with decay,
   As through a leafless landscape flows a river.

Therefore I hope, as no unwelcome guest,
   At your warm firesides, when the lamps are lighted,
To have my place reserved among the rest,
   Nor stand as one unsought, or uninvited.

LONGFELLOW.

# PREFACE.

As little idea can be gathered from the disconnected letters published in the newspapers of the daily adventures and occupations of soldiers engaged in an active campaign in India, I venture to put before the public a faithful record of the services and sufferings of one portion of the army occupied in the suppression of the mutiny; and I trust that I shall be pardoned if occasionally I am tempted to touch upon points which may seem beyond a woman's province.

That which struck me most in India was the great distance which still seems to separate that country from England, and the necessity for drawing them closer together. We frequently met with persons high in rank, both civil and military, who said, " I have not been home for twenty years : " " it is now nearly thirty years I was in England." To these men, English thoughts and English ways

are a sealed book; they have remained in India until
they have almost ceased to be Englishmen; and
should they eventually go "home," they will find
themselves as it were in a foreign land, without
friends, and without an object to live for.   Surely, if
some arrangement were made by which our countrymen in India could escape for a time to their native
air, without losing by the indulgence, the Government would benefit by the additional energy they
would throw into their work after being invigorated
by the life-giving breezes of Scotch highlands and
English downs.   Brigadier General Jacob, in his
pamphlet on "The Native Army of India, its Organi-
zation and Discipline," suggests a means by which
the number of sick furloughs might be materially
reduced, if not done away with.   "Let us," he says,
"have recourse to a principle as old as the history
of man—the institution of the Sabbath.  .  .  .  .
My proposal is to give every officer every seventh
year to himself, if he wishes to avail himself of the
indulgence; to allow him, during that period, to
go wherever it might please him to go, whether
in India, or any other part of the world.   To allow
him, during that year, to receive his full Indian
pay and allowances, to retain his staff appointment,
if he held one; but, during his absence, not to

receive the staff salary, which would go to the officer who might officiate until his return. . . . . If an officer chose to allow his sabbath to pass by and to wait until he had served twelve years, he should be allowed two years' rest on furlough; after eighteen years' uninterrupted work, three years should be allowed, and so on. . . . . The amount of vigour infused into India by this means would be incredible. . . . . The continual return to England, and reflux into India of the tide of Europeans, would be to the body moral and politic exactly what the circulation of the blood would be to the animal body. . . . . England would be our lungs, the old blood would be there aërated, and new life, health, and strength thereby sent flowing vigorously to every corner and extremity of our empire. Energy and health would take the place of languor and disease."

How many prematurely old men with cadaverous faces, sunken eyes, and hollow cheeks have we seen to whom the sabbatical year would have been a boon indeed!

Before any real good can be effected in India, that country must be brought nearer to England. The officers must have more frequent furloughs on advantageous terms. Able men from England

must be induced to travel through the country and
to accept some of the higher appointments, by reduced terms of service.  The Company's rule has
done many good things, although not as many as
it might have done; nor was their system free from
grave faults: but as for civilising, and educating,
and converting the natives of India, we must first
set an example of consistent Christianity ourselves.
We must show them that Englishmen, being Chris-
tians, cannot lie, deceive, bully, or oppress.  And
when we throw our Christianity, and consequent
superiority, in their teeth on every occasion, we
must recollect that we are dealing with a people
whose religious faith actuates them every hour of
the day.

India presents a magnificent field for work, with
a prospect of vast and noble results; and it is impossible not to feel the deepest interest in everything
connected with it; but if we desire to maintain our
supremacy, it will not be enough to vindicate our
mastership by force of arms: we must also prove
our moral superiority, and make that superiority
an evident and incontrovertible fact.

# CAMPAIGNING EXPERIENCES.

## CHAPTER I.

"Look not mournfully into the past: it cometh not again.
Wisely improve the present; it is thine. Go forth to meet
the shadowy future, without fear, and with a manly heart."

LONGFELLOW.

" The mighty wind arises, roaring seaward,
And I go."

TENNYSON.

ON the 11th May, 1856, the 8th K. R. I. Hussars
disembarked at Portsmouth, to be inspected by the
Queen, on their return from the Crimea, and on
the 8th October, 1857, the magnificent steam-ship
*Great Britain,* John Gray, Captain, left Cork Harbour for Bombay, having on board the 8th Hussars,
17th Lancers, and fifty men and several officers of
the 56th Regiment. The wind, which had blown a
hurricane on the 7th, was still raging in our teeth
as we steamed out of Queenstown, and the heavy,
confused sea made the ship labour hard to keep
her way, and sent us all to our cabins. The violent

B

rolling continued until we had passed the current
running through the Gut of Gibraltar.    But as we
followed our southern course the sea became tranquil, and the manifold beauties of tropical days and
nights gradually unfolded themselves—days all gold
and nights all silver.    Our ship spread her white
wings and sailed slowly and gracefully over the
foam-flecked, sparkling waves.    Each cavalry regiment had brought its band, refreshed with new instruments since their return from the Crimea; and
from half-past two until four o'clock their music
completed the luxury of the day.    Life on board
ship becomes so listless and so objectless, that those
who have been accustomed to exercise and activity
usually suffer both in health and temper.    Fortunately for us there was no lack of books, for the
East India Company, with praiseworthy liberality,
had sent on board five hundred volumes for the use
of the troops, and the officers of each regiment had
previously provided themselves with a goodly store.

When the *Great Britain* had been ten days at sea
we came in sight of the Islands of the Cape de Verde,
where we stopped for two days and a half to take in
coals.    Noah from the windows of the ark did not
look forward to being on land again with greater
eagerness than we; and like Noah we stood upon a
rock.    St. Vincent is of volcanic formation; no
vegetation clothes it, no flowers bloom on it.    Save
where the mists fold the rugged hills in gauzy drapery

they stand scorched and bare, as though blasted by a
curse.   The island is a large coal depôt for steam-
ships, and the few inhabitants were all at work upon
the wharf.   The English consul, sole European
resident, superintends the working of the coal-yards,
and judging from his appearance he is contented with
the station in which Providence has placed him.   An
American sloop-of-war was lying in the centre of
the picturesque harbour, and a Sardinian merchant
steamer bound for Genoa came in from Rio Janeiro;
she had on board one of the Princes Buonaparte,
mortally sick of consumption, who sent a message to
the *Great Britain* requesting medical aid.   A depu-
tation of doctors, of whom we had eight, waited on
him, and enforced his prayers to be put ashore.   The
Sardinian skipper, doubtless with an eye to his effects,
resisted his removal to the utmost of his power, but
nevertheless the poor sufferer was committed to the
goodness of the English consul.   The relief, however,
was too late; for next morning, as we left the harbour,
the consular flag was floating half-mast high.

For the next fortnight one bright day wore away
as its predecessor had done, with sunshine, monotony,
and music, when suddenly as we were sitting dream-
ing on the after part of the deck, and the men forward were amusing themselves with games and
songs, the cry of " A man overboard!" was taken
up from mouth to mouth, till, in an instant, it surged
from end to end of the ship.   Rushing to the side,

we saw him flash by underneath the stern, and drift away almost before thought could suggest a life buoy. Colonel Morris sprang to one, cut it loose, and flung it over: but could the poor struggling wretch see it? or seeing, could he reach it? The captain now strode up the deck, and with him came hope. His enormous voice soared above the surging noise. " Cram down the helm ! " " Lower away the gig ! " and down the boat went from her davits, like a live thing, and manned by five hands soon reached the drowning man. Soon in reality, but it appeared long to us. The poor man was found floating on the life buoy, and was hauled alive, but insensible, into the boat, and brought on board in safety. He was a soldier of the 14th Light Dragoons going out to join his regiment, and having climbed into the rigging to overlook the amusements on deck, he had missed his footing, and so fell overboard.

Our captain had no intention of stopping at the Cape of Good Hope, but wished, by standing away towards the American coast, to fall in with the trade winds, and so to pass some three or four hundred miles south of the Cape. We did, in fact, stand over until we neared the island of Trinidad, but the winds would do nothing but coquette. One day they blew shyly—the next day not at all—then they blew all round our sails, filling them one moment and backing them the next: so that the heavy consumption of coal rendered it imperative to take in a fresh supply, and

the ship's head was turned, with much grumbling on
the part of her officers, and great joy on that of the
troops, towards Table Bay, where we cast anchor
on the 17th November, thirty-eight days from England. We had heard so much of the heavy seas that
run into this anchorage, and of the difficulty of
getting to and from the shore, that our anticipations
were a good deal damped when on the evening before
our arrival the wind blew stiffly from the north-west.
But the next morning neither wind nor swell ruffled
the calm surface of the sea, and every one of the
officers, except the few detained on duty, went ashore.
Cape Town was the first English colony I had ever
seen, and I was agreeably surprised at the half-
foreign, half-English aspect of the place. There
were Dutch-built houses surrounded by English
railings, and pretty gardens with pomegranate hedgerows. The streets looked painfully new and un-
finished, but the trees planted before the houses gave
a pleasant aspect to the town. There were hotels
kept on English principles by Dutch landlords, Han-
som cabs driven by Caffres, with their heads tied up
in pocket-handkerchiefs, or dressed in wide-awakes
with plumes of ostrich feathers—while coming in
from the country were the teams of mules, and the
famous spans of bullocks, often twenty in a span,
driven with the stock-whip, which—long and lithe as
a salmon-rod — rarely touches its victim without
leaving a crimson trace—Caffre women with rece-

ding foreheads and projecting mouths — English
settlers riding into town like gentlemen-farmers on a
market day, or driving in shegrums with a pair of
horses harnessed curricle fashion.   As we wished
to see something of the country, riding and driving
parties were quickly organized.   We selected a nice-
looking barouche, with four fresh, well-matched little
Cape horses, and were soon flying through clouds of
dust along a broad and sandy road, with an English
turnpike (toll one shilling), and so away into the
country, our pretty leaders playing and biting at each
other as they sprang along.   We shot past hedgerows
of cactus, some bearing a pink and others a yellow
flower—past pomegranates with their scarlet bells—
past stiff and stately aloes, and little wax-like heather
—past English houses buried in deep foliage—past
little fair-haired, blue-eyed children, playing with
little natives black as coals—past a poor, blind black
beggar, sitting with uncovered head like blind Bartimeus by the wayside—and at last going up one
sharp hill at a gallop and down another at a trot,
we came to the level plain and the smooth lawns on
which stand Mr. Cloëte's house and the vineyard of
Constantia.   We inspected the large vats ranged
round rooms on the ground floor, tasted and bought
some wine, and wandered into the garden to gather
the magnificent oranges from the overloaded trees.
We afterwards proceeded to " Deep river," where we
found a large and comfortable country hotel, and saw

a famous old Cape horse, formerly the wonder of his
time, and even now a beautiful animal, and also one
or two foxhounds, part of the pack which the Irish
stable-keeper told us was farmed out during the summer months. It was difficult, on the 17th November,
to take in the idea of hounds being farmed out for the
summer, but at the Cape, Christmas Day is often the
hottest of the year. I filled my hands with oleanders,
lilies, pomegranates, arums, and roses, and twined a
wreath of passion-flowers amongst the feathers of my
hat. We then resumed our places in the carriage,
and as it was verging towards evening we returned
to Cape Town, not forgetting " Bartimeus" as we
passed. Our driver did not bait his horses the whole
day, nor even wash out their mouths. I suggested
it to him, but he said it was not the custom; and however long the journey, the horse was never refreshed
until it was over. At the *table d'hôte* at Parke's
Hotel, where we dined, we met some officers of the
98th, bound to Kurrachee, landed from on board the
steam-ship *Ireland*, which had been fifty-four days
out. We spent two whole days on shore, and the
second we devoted to riding round the Table Mountain, and enjoying, as much as the intolerable dust
would permit, the lovely and extensive view of sea
and land. In the harbour was every imaginable
species of craft, from the *Himalaya* to the light fishing barque of Cape Town. The *Great Britain* and
*Himalaya* had never been side by side before, and

owing to the tremendous spars and heavy rigging of
the *Great Britain*, she, although in reality some few
feet shorter, appeared the larger of the two.

> " Oh how yon argosies, with portly sail,
> Like signiors and rich burghers of the flood—
> Or, as it were, the pageants of the sea,
> Did overpeer the petty traffickers
> That curtsied to them reverence,
> As they flew by them with their woven wings."

The inland view, when we could clear out our
eyes to see it, was extensive and fine, and the flowers
most fragrant and refreshing; but the strong wind
and storms of dust made us glad to hasten to our
Inn, where I found, on consulting my glass, that my
hair and face were of an uniform brick red. We
afterwards went to the stables of Mr. Kaien Meyer,
from which our horses of this and the previous day
had been furnished. He showed us a fine three-year
old bright bay horse, over fifteen hands, and very
powerful. We were half inclined to purchase, but
considering the risk of transport to Bombay and
the long price asked, we thought it more prudent
to decline — a decision we had afterwards no cause
to regret. The next morning we were awakened
by the rain beating heavily against our windows.
As the *Great Britain* was to go out of Table Bay
at twelve o'clock, it was important to lose no time
in engaging a large and sea-worthy boat, for the
waves often rise to such an extent as to render it
impossible to leave the shore. Many a captain of

a vessel has stood on the pier and seen his ship
standing out to sea, to avoid being driven on the
rocks, while he has offered 100*l.* or even 200*l.* to
the boatmen to put him on board; and offered it
in vain. The wind and the sea were both much
rougher than was pleasant; but we fortunately fell
in with some of our friends who had engaged a large
sailing-boat, and we secured two places in her.
We sprang into the boat, from the pier-head, as she
rose on the waves, and after some little confusion,
got under weigh. We went on very well for those
who like boating in a storm, which I confess I do
not, until we neared the ship, when the danger of
keeping the boat alongside the gangway ladder, and
the difficulty of springing from the gunwale of the
boat to the ladder, called into requisition all one's
self-control. However, at last all were safely re-
embarked, though not without some very narrow
escapes; and we then hove anchor, and put out into
a rough and disagreeable sea.

The *Himalaya,* which had been sent to the Cape
from Bombay for a cargo of horses for the use of
the troops, brought the tidings of the fall of Delhi.
We had been so long unable to obtain Indian news,
that we felt inclined to overrate the value of what
now reached us. We fancied that with the taking
of Delhi the chief part of the mutiny was crushed,
and that the rebels would never attempt resistance
any more. To the seekers for military distinction,

the news was unwelcome, as they feared the work would be over before they arrived.   One officer, especially, to whom the smoke of the cannon was as the breath of life, would chafe at the tardy motion of the ship that held him back from the tented field ; little knowing that she was bearing him, the strong, the gentle, the bravest of the brave, true Christian, true soldier, and true friend, not into the pomp and circumstance of war, not to contested fields, and the thunder of the guns, but to long and weary sickness—to a wasting of energy, and strength, and hope, and to his death and burial!  So mercifully does a good Providence veil the future from our eyes.

The first few days after leaving the Cape were disagreeable, and cold, and rough ; and the *Great Britain* rolled about, as if she had uneasy dreams, although from her great size and breadth of beam, she went through the seas more easily than a smaller craft.   This was the most uncomfortable part of our voyage.   By and by the sky cleared, and the waves became blue, and the Indian Ocean opened out before us—an expanse of unutterable calm.

> " All round the ship the languid air did swoon,
>   Breathing like one that hath a weary dream."

Scarcely a ripple moved the surface of the lake-like sea.   Mr. Chapman, our chief mate, who had been attacked by sickness, and whose absence was re-

gretted both as an amusing companion and as an
admirable seaman, now resumed his place on deck,
to the especial delectation of "Toby," a little spaniel
which had come on board with the 17th Lancers.
We began to suffer very much from the heat of the
weather, which made it almost impossible to remain
in the saloon or the cabin. The thermometer hanging in our cabin (which being nearly always on the
weather side, was one of the coolest in the ship)
ranged, from the 3rd December to the 16th, at from
74° to 88°; but it was remarked that on each occasion of our crossing the line, the day was unusually
cool and agreeable.

At length our voyage began to draw near its
completion. It had been a weary time for all of
us, though perhaps less so for me than for others,
as I could occasionally find occupation in needle-
work. But it was with feelings of regret that I
thought of leaving the ship, where so much consideration and kindness had been shown me. I had
begun the voyage in much unhappiness at having
so soon again to leave England, and to separate
myself not only from my relations, but from all
my household gods. The parting from attached
servants, from horses, which one learns to love so
much—from the pet dog, gift of one now lying beneath
the rose-coloured plain of Balaklava, had each a separate pain. The beauties of tropical sea and sky, however, had turned my thoughts from the past to the

present: the contemplation of the present braced my spirits, and I gradually learnt to unwind my heart from England, to which it had for a second time begun to cling, and to allow it to anticipate its Indian future. To England shall I ever again return? Was my last short sojourn there but the opening chord of a *nunc dimittis,* bidding me depart in peace from it for ever? My house there is set in order: the rest is at the ordering of Him " who holdeth our lives in His hand."

In spite of the sunshine, three days before our arrival at Bombay, a gloom fell upon us, owing to the death of one of the men of the 17th Lancers from rheumatism affecting the heart. Up to a late hour on the previous evening, the doctors entertained a hope that he would recover, or, at any rate, linger for some time; but at five o'clock the following morning he expired, and was buried between ten and eleven o'clock the same day. The quiet of the calm and shining sea robbed his grave of its horror. This was the first and only casualty of our otherwise prosperous voyage. Throughout his burial day the wind was calm and the sea at rest. Next morning, a very strong breeze sprang up from the north-east, dead ahead of the ship, retarding her way so much that all hope of saving the Bombay mail, which we believed left on the 17th, was at an end. The captain was extremely desirous to reach Bombay before its departure, in order that his ship might be reported at Lloyd's as having arrived. In that event, she would have made her outward voyage in seventy days, which she was bound under heavy penalties to do. On Tuesday evening, after we had abandoned all expectation of reaching Bombay on the Thursday, the wind dropped, and the sea grew calm. Every furnace (eighteen, I believe) was a-light; the ship throbbed from stem to stern, like an over-driven horse; her waste pipes gasped and sobbed, and every yard was braced up, so as to offer least resistance to the air. After dinner, the health of Captain Gray was given with many just expressions of regard, and the cheers from the saloon were taken up by the men on deck. The ship still strained and panted forwards, making such good way during the night, that at breakfast next morning, we were greeted with the cheerful news, " We shall drop anchor in Bombay Harbour this afternoon at four o'clock ; completing our voyage in seventy days from England, and sixty-four under steam." The Indian shore lay on our starboard side—red, arid, parched, and bare. We traced it with interest all the morning, following its outlines on the chart. About half-past two, we came in sight of Bombay, and also of the ship *Arabia*, Captain Forrest, an old Crimean friend, which was lying becalmed, with her head towards Bombay. About three o'clock, we took a pilot on board, and soon after four were at anchor in the harbour, and learnt to our great joy that the mail did not leave until the 18th, so that plenty of time remained for the ship to be reported, and for letters to be posted to our friends. The ship rested. The colonels of the 8th Hussars and 17th Lancers came on board, and from them we heard that the interior of India was still very gravely disturbed; and that so far from being stationed in cantonments, one if not both of the regiments would have to march immediately. Early on the following day, the 8th disembarked, and encamped on the esplanade; and on the next morning, the 17th landed, and proceeded at once by railway towards Kirkee.

# CHAPTER II.

"In a strange land,
Strange things, however trivial, reach the heart,
And through the heart the head; clearing away
The narrow notions that grow up at home."

ROGERS.

"That day we gave
To pleasure, and, unconscious of their flight,
Another and another."

*Ibid.*

ON Saturday, 19th December, my husband and I
left the *Great Britain* and established ourselves in a
large tent in the garden of the Hope Hall Hotel at
Mazagon, near Bombay, preferring the open air and
sunshine to the close rooms of a crowded house. On
landing at the Apollo Bunder, we found no other
conveyance was to be got, so I satisfied some clamor-
ous natives by allowing them to carry me in a
" palki." The motion was easy, and the attitude
luxurious; but the idea of transforming my fellow-
creatures into beasts of burden was repugnant to
me, and at the first halting-place I dismissed the
" palki " and waited until a carriage was procured.
I could not believe that the time would come, when I
should gladly travel in a palanquin for miles; being

too much prostrated with pain and weakness to
sit in my saddle, or to endure the motion of a carriage.  My first impression on entering Bombay was
one of disappointment.  One saw nothing but native
houses with wooden fronts and deep projecting roofs
leaning over unpaved streets; and open shops, as in
a Turkish bazar, with here and there the funniest
Parsee names, written in English characters.  Nearly
all the English residents live outside the town, on
Malabar Hill, in bungalows, more or less capacious
and handsome.  The part of Bombay near the sea
is strongly fortified; and immediately outside the
fort is the esplanade where the 8th Hussars, and the
95th Regiment, were encamped.  This is the place
of fashionable resort, where from half-past four until
seven o'clock may be seen every equipage and horse
in Bombay, and some of the latter are magnificent.
Near the esplanade is a large native quarter, densely
populated and very squalid.  In the country just
beyond are the Byculla Club, the church, the race-
course, and the houses of the wealthy merchants,
both English and Parsee.

The officers of the 17th Lancers, during the few
hours which they spent in Bombay previous to their
departure for Kirkee, endeavoured at any cost to
provide themselves with horses.  Never had the
native dealers such a golden harvest.  " A thousand
rupees," " two thousand rupees," were words familiar
to their mouths; so much so, that they forgot all

intermediate numerals.    The enormous demand and
the very inadequate supply, enabled them to obtain
almost any price they liked to ask.

The soldiers encamped on the esplanade are loud
in their praises of Indian life.    The large roomy
tents, and numerous native servants, contrast pleasantly enough with their Crimean experiences.    The
officers' tents, double-walled and roofed, with a bath-
room adjoining and grass or wire-woven doors,
appear to possess every means of comfort, and at
this present season, the 28th December, the climate
is absolutely perfect.    The mornings and evenings
are cool and breezy, noonday is excessively hot; and
during the few days we have as yet passed in India,
I have not seen a cloud.    The glory of the sunsets
fills the mind with wonder and admiration; nor can
I feel astonished at the Parsee who prostrates himself on the sea-shore, with his face towards the
declining sun.    The number of servants requisite to
form a moderate Indian establishment differs very
materially from English notions.    We found it necessary to engage a head servant or butler, who is in
fact the house-steward, and provides for the household and horses; a second servant or bearer, who
attends to the master as personal servant, and waits
at table with the butler; a cook; a mapaul, who
cleans lamps, plates, knives and forks; a bheestie,
or water-carrier: a dhobie, or washerman; a dirsee,
or tailor, to repair the ruthless damages done by the

dhobie; a tent lascar, to pitch the tent; a gari-
wallah, to drive the covered bullock shegrum, which
it is necessary to have for going out in the sun; and,
lastly, a ghorawallah for each horse. I could not
understand at first how so large an establishment
would be transported on the march, but time, which
teaches many things, showed me that without each
and every man of them, it was next to impossible to
move at all: and in India an army of 10,000 men is
reckoned to have not less than 30,000 camp followers—a number which would have astonished
Julius Cæsar.

A thermometer showing 80° at noon made us
almost doubt the possibility of its being New Year's
Day, with which our associations are of clear frosty
atmosphere and ice-bound ponds and fields. Every
bell on shore and in harbour kept up a merry peal,
and the guns of the fort saluted at daybreak. How
little we thought as the last new year dawned upon us
through clouds and nipping wind, that before another
came we should be basking beneath an Indian sun.
But—

"All that moveth doth in change delight."

And now that the voyage is over, I cannot but be
glad that this new phase of life opens before me. We
are at present established in the lines of the regiment
on the esplanade, in a large double-walled and
double-roofed tent, sixteen feet long by fourteen
wide, which, with carpets, arm-chairs, tables, lamps,

and a pianoforte, is comfortable enough. Opening
from this is a baychuba, or tent without a pole, fitted
up as a sleeping-room, while beyond the baychuba
and also opening into it, is the bath-room. The
servants' tents are pitched in the rear, and the horses
are picketted close by. Each horse has his own
ghorawallah, or syce (Anglicè groom), sitting near
his head all day and sleeping close to him at night.
The Arab horses are, with few exceptions, as tame as
English pet dogs: they never start back from the
hand as do English horses reared in stalls and badly
treated by their grooms, nor do they object to the
handling of their hind legs, by which they are
hobbled.

In our search for horses we have had to visit the
various dealers' yards. We went first to Mahomet
Bouker's stables, where upwards of a thousand
horses were ranged under open sheds. These, however, were of inferior caste, and had already been
selected for the ranks of various regiments. A
large-boned chesnut horse hid in a dark corner
caught our attention. "His price is a thousand
rupees," said the courteous Mahomet; "shall I have
him run out for you?" He appeared accordingly, and
was such a veteran that we could not refrain from
laughing at the estimate placed on our knowledge of
horseflesh; so we bowed, and walked out of the yard.
Our next visit was to Dhady, whose horses, fewer in
number, were mostly new arrivals from shipboard,

and in very poor condition. Of him we purchased "The Pearl." Fukergee's stables, consisting of rows of loose boxes, next claimed our attention, and several horses were examined and tried without success, until one day he brought "The Rajah" down to camp.

My husband's stud, which is now complete, consists of "The Rajah," his first charger, a very handsome mottled Arab four-year old, with black mane and tail, as full of tricks as a monkey, and half inclined, if not well managed, to become vicious; his second charger, a strong white Arab, which speedily became a great favourite—a powerful dark iron grey, with large, black, good-tempered eyes, and the sweetest disposition in the world, which soon learnt to know his name of "Prince," and of which I immediately took possession for my own riding; and lastly, my little nutmeg grey, deservedly called "The Pearl,"—slight, wiry, active, showy, full of life and fire, of which I am the more proud, as I broke him in myself, and no one else has ever been upon his back.

A few nights after our arrival we were invited by a Parsee merchant of some consideration to a nautch, given in honour of his son's wedding; and, being curious as to the customs of the richer natives, we accepted the invitation and went at about ten P.M. We drove to the entrance of a courtyard, which was roofed in with drapery of white cloth, spangled with stars,

and hung with gold tinsel fringe. On a raised plat-
form was the band of the 8th Hussars, lent for the
occasion. Ascending the staircase, we found ourselves in a long room, beautifully lighted by numerous
chandeliers; round the walls were ranged nearly a
hundred guests, Mussulmans, Hindoos, Parsees, and
a few Englishmen. The natives were dressed in
white, with gorgeous turbans, each guest holding a
bouquet and a fan. The effect of these gay colours
was light and happy to a great degree, and contrasted well with our heavy uniforms, fastened to the
chin, and ponderous with gold lace. As soon as we
arrived we were sprinkled with rose-water and presented with betel-nut, a bouquet, and a fan. The
Hussar band speedily ceased playing, and the nautch
dancers took possession of the floor. Two young
women, in magnificent dresses, with diamond rings
in their noses and silver anklets, commenced a slow
and monotonous dance, marking time by a nasal song,
most disagreeable to the ear. They were accompanied by two men, one playing a kind of banjo, and
the other beating a tom-tom. There was neither
grace in the dance nor harmony in the song. The
whole entertainment was hot and tedious; and we
left soon after midnight, in spite of the protestations
of our host that the dancing would continue until
four or five o'clock. Several Parsees present conversed with me in English, and one evinced curiosity
to know if the spectacle I was witnessing bore any

resemblance to an English ball.    On mentioning this
to a friend a day or two after, I was told that at one
of the Governor's balls a Hindoo, after watching the
dancers for some time, expressed his intention of
" sending to England for a ball."    He imagined that
the guests were exhibitors for money, and that he
could purchase some equally good for a specified
outlay.

Shortly before our arrival at Bombay, two sepoys
of the Native Infantry stationed there had been
blown away from guns, and a third was transported
for life.    As far as we can judge, the disaffection
does not appear likely to spread—the rebels being
overawed by the rapid arrival of European troops.
At the time these two executions took place, the
English military force in Bombay did not exceed two
hundred men, while a regiment of Native Infantry,
numbering eleven hundred, was encamped on the
esplanade.    The two hundred, however, proved sufficient to maintain order until reinforcements, hastily
sent for to the Mauritius and elsewhere, arrived.    Of
course, various opinions are expressed by the residents.    Some imagine that the mutineers are only
awaiting the dispersion of the troops to rise *en masse*
and murder every English man, woman, and child in
Bombay; while others maintain that the disaffection
is purely military, and is even now crushed, as far as
Bombay is concerned.    In the midst of these con-
flicting hopes and fears, an unexpected demonstration

has been made in our favour by the wealthy Parsee residents and merchants, headed by Cursetjee Jejeebhoy, the eldest son of Sir Jamsetjee. The whole of the newly-arrived English forces, officers and men, together with the Governor, the Commander-in-Chief, and all the principal officers, civil, military, and naval, have been invited to a vast banquet on the esplanade. A line of lofty tents, extending for more than a quarter of a mile, and surrounded by temporary walls, has been erected for the banquet, and another range of the same extent for the ball-room and supper. The invitation was accepted without much cordiality on the part of the troops, who cannot understand accepting an entertainment from the natives of a country, the soil of which is stained with the blood of English men, women, and children.

Upwards of two thousand men and officers sat down to dinner. All wore either swords or side-arms; and a strong guard was left in camp. The speeches made during the entertainment by the Parsees were most friendly, and I wish I had space to record that of Lord Elphinstone.

No ladies were invited to the dinner; but when the tents appropriated to dancing were thrown open, I was astonished and surprised at their scanty attendance. Amongst the throng of Englishmen, French naval officers, and Americans, there was scarcely a score of ladies, and these I know had hard battles to fight with the prejudices of the rest of the female community. I fancy a fear of losing caste in society, or offending against some ill-defined point of etiquette, deterred many. For on all questions of etiquette the Indian ladies are particular to a curious and amusing degree. The pertinacity with which claims for precedence are maintained, where there is not a shade of difference in the rank, or rather no rank, of the guests, is very entertaining to a new comer. I am told that it is often most difficult to give precedence to one without direfully offending all the rest. According to the custom here, the lady who takes precedence must be the first to break up the party; and until she leaves no other guest can quit the room. I witnessed an amusing instance of the consequences of this stringent law. We were dining at a friend's house, when a lady was taken suddenly ill. The " senior lady" (in regimental phrase) had shown no symptoms of departure. The case was urgent. The mistress of the house represented it; and the difficulty was solved by the lady who took precedence rising and making her adieux; but as her carriage was not in waiting, she retired to the empty dining-room, where she sat in state in the dark until it arrived!

Notwithstanding their strict obedience to etiquette, I cannot say that I found the manners of my fellow-countrywomen in India characterized by real politeness. On one occasion we were dining at the house of the highest person in the presidency, himself re-

markable for his courtesy. The guests, about seventy
in number, were nearly all strangers to me; and
during that *triste* period after dinner devoted by the
ladies to the exclusive enjoyment of each other's
society, I heard the question asked across the room,
" Which is Mrs. Duberly?" and as loudly replied to
by, " There she is, sitting on the sofa, in pink," with
the comment from a third of, " Oh! is that the
Crimean heroine? "—while two young ladies shifted
their chairs, in order to take an inventory of me at
their leisure.

Intelligence from the interior reaches us very
much as the Crimean news did at Balaklava, viz.,
through the columns of the English newspapers.
Neither the local papers nor the people of Bombay
appear to give themselves much concern about the
turmoil of the northern states. Balls and dinner
parties succeed each other rapidly; and I never
remember to have seen a more beautiful ball-room,
or one better adapted to its purpose, than that at
Bombay.

Our stay here will be no longer than is necessary
to enable us to procure tents, servants, and a few
horses for the officers and men, as we have received
final orders to embark for Mandavee, in Cutch, on
Saturday, 23rd January. The Calcutta papers, received on the 22nd, contain an account of the reception of the wounded men and widows and orphans
from Lucknow. A royal salute was fired in their

honour; and they were met on landing by sympathizing crowds, eager with their offers of shelter and assistance.    Too late! too late! no sympathy can heal such wounds, no friendship can restore the murdered dead.    When I think upon this terrible insurrection, and recollect how deeply the rebels have stained themselves with English blood, the blood of English women and of little helpless children, I can only look forward with awe to the day of vengeance, when our hands shall be dipped in the blood of our enemies, and the tongues of our dogs shall be red through the same.

On Thursday the 21st, the heavy baggage, mess-stores, &c., were embarked.    On Friday, the horses and the rest of the baggage followed; and on Saturday we went on board the steam-ship *Khersonese*, and at four o'clock in the afternoon, after Lieut.-Col. Wilmer, who was found to be suffering from small-pox, had been put on shore, we took the *Persia* in tow, and steamed out of Bombay harbour, bound for Mandavee.

# CHAPTER III.

"What mortal in the world, if without inward calling he take
up a trade, an art, or any other mode of life, will not find his
situation miserable ?   But he who is born with capacities for any
undertaking, finds in executing it the fairest portion of his being.
Nothing upon earth without its difficulties !   It is the secret
impulse within, it is the love and delight we feel, that help us to
conquer obstacles, to clear out new paths, to overleap the bounds
of that narrow circle in which others poorly toil."
WILHELM MEISTER.

WE had watched most anxiously for the mail which
was due on the 22nd of January, but it did not arrive
before we left Bombay.   Unless delayed by an accident the steam-boat must have come in a few hours
afterwards, so that the disappointment was doubly
keen.   How little can the daily letter-writers of
England imagine the eagerness with which exiles in
a far country look forward to the arrival of the post,
bringing them news from home.   To us letters from
England are like voices from another world.

Bombay Harbour lay serene in the evening twilight as we sat on deck and watched until we could
no longer discern the houses and the cathedral tower.
Fatigue drove me early to my cabin : but not to
sleep.   We had been late in going on board, and

found that the only vacant cabin was the one next to that from which poor Colonel Wilmer had been removed. I went into it, not without a shiver—and the thought of small-pox, combined with extreme fatigue and the attacks of hordes of ferocious insects, deprived me of all sleep. Next morning a head wind sprang up, retarding our course very seriously. In addition to the smoke from the funnel sweeping over the after-part of the vessel, and filling our lungs with gas, we found the crowds of native servants and camp followers who encumbered the decks anything but fragrant. The *Persia*, a ship of 1,700 tons, was a sad drag on engines not over strong; and what with bad cooking, undrinkable tea, and detestable wine, we experienced as many disagreeables as could well be crammed into so short a voyage. On the morning of Wednesday the 27th, we were shown a long line of flat sandy coast, with a small town on the shore, apparently distant about nine or ten miles. We watched it assiduously from nine A. M. until three P. M., but without making any perceptible approach. The current and the wind were strong against us; and the water was so shallow that both ships were compelled to sound incessantly. About half-past four o'clock we cast anchor two miles from the shore, but at that distance it was too late to commence disembarking horses. Next morning business began in earnest, but several men and officers, and nearly all the horses, remained on board that night also. At one time it was intended to send us to Gogeh, a seaport in the Gulf of Cambay, but the landing there proved to be even worse than at Mandavee. We found that there would be no difficulty as to transport as far as Bhooj, thirty-six miles distant, and to that place the dismounted squadrons were to march on foot.

On Friday, the 29th January, may be said to have commenced our Indian campaign. We left the *Khersonese* in a large native boat, with several of the soldiers. It was very rough, and the old boat, which must have been built time out of mind, lurched and groaned to a surprising extent. It did not reassure us to hear that a hundred and fifty pilgrims had been drowned two days before out of a similar boat; however, after a great deal of screaming and jabber on the part of the native crew, we stuck fast on a sand-bank, and were carried to the beach. The landing is so bad for horse-boats at this place that a whole boat-load, arriving after the turn of the tide, were knocking about all night; unfortunately our horses were of the number, and as none of them had been fed since the previous morning, we found them on our arrival in camp in a great state of exhaustion, and indeed one was so weak that we feared for his life. Our tents were pitched upon the sea-shore, in deep sand, which was all very well for the transport camels, but very disagreeable to us. I was particularly struck with the difference between an Indian town and the cities I had previously seen in European and Asiatic

Turkey. A traveller who has seen one Turkish town has seen them all. The same narrow and filthy streets, the same figures sitting in the same attitude, in large open shop windows, shaded by a lifted shutter stretching across the street, the same cats and dogs, and the same graceful minarets that are in Constantinople, may be seen more or less in every Turkish town.

The aspect of an Indian town is different; the domed temple of the Hindoo stands out in greater prominence than the airy minaret of the Mussulman. Hideous little carved gods, daubed with red paint, are exposed to public view in wayside temples, like the shrines of the Virgin and the Saints in a Continental town. On certain days these idols are fresh painted and dressed in fine clothes; when devout worshippers appear with mud and rice upon their foreheads, or with bars of white and red mud upon their cheeks. This mud, which comes, I believe, from the Ganges, the Sacred River, is worn as a religious emblem, and is hard to reconcile with our European ideas of beautiful adornment. The greater part of the inhabitants of Mandavee are Banyans and Jains, whose creed forbids the destruction of life. No living creature is destroyed in the town. The fish near it swim unconscious of the hook; cows, being sacred, are of course exempt from injury; whoever shoots a peacock must pay a fine of 500 rupees, or 50l. Parrots, hawks, crows, and sheep

all live as long as nature will permit; but at a
village a few miles distant, sheep, fowls, and fish
are purchaseable. The hawks, conscious of security,
come swooping over the camp kitchens, and carry
off pieces of meat, almost from between the fingers
of the cooks. At Bombay there is a hospital close
to the sea for maimed, diseased, or aged animals,
whither they are brought to await the approach of
death. Horses, and other animals, suffering from
whatever cause, are there left to linger until nature
puts a period to their pain, instead of being mercifully and instantaneously destroyed. The principle
is good, which teaches men to refrain from taking
God's great gift of life; but I saw enough of animal
suffering in the Crimea, to teach me that death is
often the greater blessing. In consequence of this
local protection the neighbourhood of Mandavee
abounds in game of almost every kind. The Rao of
Cutch has a dirty-looking and dilapidated palace
here in which his eldest son occasionally resides.
Writing of palaces reminds me of something we
heard when at Bombay regarding the capture of
Delhi. The army which took the place after fearful
loss and great hardships, imagined that when the
city fell, everything in it would be theirs. Great
was their surprise and disappointment when they
found that plunder was most strictly forbidden,
and that instead of booty each man was to receive a few extra rupees. The consequence was

that chalk inscriptions were scrawled all over the town :—

"DELHI TAKEN,

AND INDIA SAVED, FOR TWENTY RUPEES."

When we heard of the fall of Delhi from the officers of the *Himalaya*, the news kindled the warlike enthusiasm of officers and men. It was imagined that the Avenger would complete his work, and that not a trace would be left of the city to show future generations where it stood. As they walked the deck, and discussed the news in groups, one of them gave utterance to the following lurid words, which, with all their savage imagery of the days of Tilley and Wallenstein, still seemed to find an echo in most soldiers' hearts :—

> " When the breach was open laid,
>   Bold we mounted to the attack ;
> Five times the assault was made ;
>   Four times we were driven back ;
> But the fifth time, up we strode
>   O'er the dying and the dead,
> Red the western sunbeams glowed,
>   Sinking in a blaze of red.
> Redder in the gory way
>   Our deep plashing footsteps sank,
> As the cry of ' Slay—slay—slay ! '
>   Echoed fierce from rank to rank.
> And we slew, and slew, and slew—
>   Slew them with unpitying sword.
> Negligently could we do
>   The commanding of the Lord ?

Fled the coward, fought the brave,
   Wept the widow, wailed the child,
But there did not scape the glaive
   Man that frowned, or babe that smiled.
There were thrice ten thousand men
   When that morning's sun arose;
Lived not thrice three hundred when
   Sunk that sun at evening's close.
Then we spread the wasting flame,
   Fed to fury by the wind ;
Of the city but the name,
   Nothing else, remained behind.
But it burned not till it gave
   All it had to yield of spoil—
Should not brave soldadoes have
   Some rewarding for their toil?
What the villein sons of trade
   Earned by years of toil and care,
Prostrate at our bidding laid,
   In one moment won was there.
Hall and palace, dome and tower,
   Lowly cot and soaring spire,
Sank in that victorious hour
   Which consigned the town to fire.
Then throughout the burning town,
   'Mid the steaming heaps of dead,
Cheered by sound of hostile moan,
   We the gorgeous banquet spread:
Laughing loud and quaffing long,
   At our glorious labour o'er,
To the skies our jocund song
   Told that Magdeburg was no more!" *

I shudder as I write these terrible lines. Alas! for
the horrors of Cawnpore, and for the retribution
which must avenge them!

---

   * Dr. MAGINN's *Taking of Magdeburg.*

# CHAPTER IV.

"In the world's broad field of battle,
In the bivouac of life,
Be not like dumb driven cattle:
Be a hero in the strife."
LONGFELLOW.

"Quale per incertam lunam sub luce malignâ
Est iter."

AT midnight on Sunday, 31st January, the *reveillée*
sounded, and by two o'clock the regiment began
its march.    The mounted column first, then the
treasure-chest on a tumbril, escorted by the dismounted men, the whole followed by an incredible
train of bullock-waggons and camels laden with
baggage.    The full moon enabled us to follow the
track through a very ugly country; but the wind
was extremely cold, and we all hailed the rising sun
with satisfaction.    Camp was pitched near the village
of Bara-Assumbia about nine o'clock, and breakfast
followed as speedily as might be.    The most energetic
of the officers took their guns, and started in quest
of game.    During these very early days of marching,
before we had become accustomed to it, the mess-
dinner was at two o'clock, and the mess-tent, and

all others that could be spared, were struck at four, and sent on overnight to the next halting-place, in charge of an officer and an advance party. The object aimed at by this arrangement was to have the tents so sent forward pitched before the regiment came in from the march, that there might be no delay for breakfast; but as the officers selected never marked out the camp until the arrival of the colonel, the plan turned out a failure. Next morning *reveillée* sounded at two A.M., and we started at four. This was a more adventurous march; for as the tumbril and baggage guards were unable to keep up with the column, at a point where the tracks became intricate, they lost their road, not easily discernible in moonlight, and the whole of the long train of baggage went astray. My husband and I were riding in the rear, and we started in different directions, in the hope of finding either the column or the road. In about an hour and a half, a track was discovered, which to our joy proved to be the right one, and, after much bumping and jolting over deep ruts and uneven ground, and many escapes from falling into holes and nullahs, the train of carts and camels eventually reached Naigpoor, about two hours after the column. Shooting was resumed with unabated vigour, several officers, who had marched on foot, going out immediately after breakfast. Major Chetwode shot a beautiful antelope, and loaded his beaters with game. The next day's

march brought us into Bhooj, where we halted for
several days.   On our arrival, Colonel Trevelyan,
Political Resident in Cutch, although a total stranger
to me, insisted, with the true spirit of hospitality,
that we should be his guests at the Residency,
instead of remaining in camp during the halt.   A
suite of handsome rooms was given up to us, and
our horses were taken in as well.   It was the
hospitality of a prince ; and arriving as we did, all
dusty, travel-stained, and fatigued, it seemed as
though we could not luxuriate enough in the comforts of a well-appointed house, with its large, cool,
lofty rooms, and refreshing baths.   Bhooj possesses
several objects of interest ; amongst which are the
tombs of the former Raos.   They are of red sand-
stone, hundreds of years old ; some having almost
crumbled away, while the one or two that remain
perfect are approached by handsome flights of steps,
and are rich in ornament as well as beautiful in
architectural design.   The domed roofs are supported
on clusters, groups, and rows of pillars ; while the
fantastic and elaborate carvings of every corner
remind the spectator of the like ornaments on our
fairest English cathedrals.   The Rao's Palace, and
also several of the tombs, are decorated with figures
resembling those seen on English monuments of
ancient date.   An equestrian statue in chain armour,
looking very like a crusader, adorns the palace : and
the entrance to the door of the largest tomb is

guarded by two figures, male and female, apparently about the date of Henry I. On inquiry, I learned that many, many years ago, a Dutch sculptor came to Bhooj, and left these traces of his skill. Conjecture wanders in vain over the history of this man. How and why he came so far, a solitary Christian outcast among the heathen, is unknown. His name has long been lost, but his memory lives in his works.

> " Here, in silence and in sorrow, toiling with a busy hand,
> Like an emigrant he wandered, seeking for the Better Land.
> 'Emigravit' is the inscription on the tombstone where he lies:
> Dead he is not, but departed—for the Artist never dies."

The second day of our halt at Bhooj was one of gloom for all of us. The post which arrived in the morning brought us the melancholy news of the death of Lieutenant-Colonel Wilmer, whom we left sick at Bombay. I have since heard that he died neglected, and almost alone. This affected us the more, as although Colonel Wilmer only joined the 8th Hussars on their arrival in India, he had won the esteem and goodwill of all. But a still heavier calamity hung over this fated day; the sportsmen went out to shoot, and with them a young Lieutenant Helme, who had joined scarcely a year ago. He became separated from the rest, and was only attended by his ghorawallah, who followed for the purpose of carrying his game. The young man had his gun over his shoulder at full cock, when his foot tripped, and he stumbled heavily. The gun flew from his hand, and struck the ground with such force that it exploded, and the contents passed through his body. The ghorawallah, sole witness of the appalling accident, said he had not time to utter a single word, but died as he fell. The terrified servant ran in haste to some of the unfortunate young man's brother officers, who were shooting near, and meeting Lieutenant the Hon. E. Stourton, brought him to where the body lay. Medical assistance and a doolie were quickly on the spot, but he was stone dead. At the inquest, held the following morning, a verdict of " accidental death" was returned; and this comfort was left to us, that he is buried in consecrated ground, and amongst his own countrymen, in the English cemetery at Bhooj, where a monument was erected to his memory by his brother officers. He was a quiet and amiable youth, and many were grieved at his untimely end.

Tidings of the evacuation of Awah reached Colonel Trevelyan while we were at the Residency. The rebels had strongly fortified it, and appeared determined to resist. While preparations were being made for the siege, a violent storm of thunder and lightning, with terrific rain, compelled the suspension of all operations; and the rebels taking advantage of the elemental din, and under cover of heaven's artillery, abandoned the fort. We heard that a hundred prisoners were made, of whom twenty-four were hanged, and one shot.

I received an intimation from the Ranees, appointing an interview with me, and was much gratified at having an opportunity of seeing the interior of an Indian court. Mrs. Jervis, the wife of the resident chaplain at Bhooj, kindly accompanied me as interpretress. The Rao sent his carriage, an English brougham, for us, with an escort both of horse and foot. The courtyard of the palace, an extensive and handsome building, was thronged with people, and music commenced as our carriage drew up at the foot of the stone steps leading to the ladies' apartments. We saw six of the Ranees, and the wife of the Rao's eldest son. The ladies, who received us in the durbar room, were seated on chairs in a row, surrounded by female attendants and musicians. They rose as we entered, and extended their hands; seats were then placed for us opposite to them. The eldest lady conversed: the rest sat by in silence. I never saw such a profusion of jewellery in my life. The forehead of each was hidden by a circular ornament of precious stones, and even their eyelids were fringed with diamonds; nose jewels, the size and weight of which distorted the nostril, completed the decorations of the face. Several necklaces, some apparently of solid gold, others of strings of pearls, covered the neck and bosom; while massive bracelets, blazing with rubies and emeralds, encircled their arms from elbow to wrist. One bracelet I particularly remember; it was a thick and heavy circlet of gold, studded with about thirty emeralds the size of peas. On their ankles they wore three or four chains and anklets of different patterns, and each toe was covered with an ornament resembling enamelled leaves. The Ranee who conversed appeared to be an unusually intelligent woman. She was well informed as to everything relating to the royal families of Europe, and listened with interest for my answers to her various questions. Mrs. Jervis mentioned that I was the Englishwoman whom the Ranee had heard of as having been with the army during the Crimean war; and her inquiries proved that she was familiar with the leading events of the campaign. Her information was, I believe, acquired from a Persian newspaper, which she receives once a week. She was very desirous to ascertain whether the men of the regiment entertained hostile feelings towards the native population, or only towards such as had revolted. The ladies examined my watch and bracelets very minutely, and then desired their attendants to show me their sleeping apartments. This was quite exceeding ordinary etiquette, and arose evidently from a wish to make their friendly feeling as manifest as possible. The rooms were dark and close, but the swinging cots were very handsome. That of the eldest Ranee was made entirely of silver, and suspended from the ceiling by massive chains, carved into elephants, horses, and palm-trees. Close to it was a smaller swinging bed, in a handsome silver frame. It was the cot which had been occupied by her son, the heir apparent, when he was a little child; and, mother-like, she still keeps it in her room. The ladies retire about ten or eleven o'clock, and are rocked and rung to sleep by little silver bells suspended from the chains that swing the cot. One thing struck me: when in conversation with the Ranee, she asked rather eagerly if I had ever been actually present at a battle. And on being answered in the affirmative, she fell back in her chair and sighed. A whole lifetime of suppressed emotion, of crushed ambition, of helplessness, and weariness, seemed to be comprehended in that short sigh.

We quitted Bhooj with great regret on the 9th February. Our first march, of sixteen miles, to Dhunnytee was not commenced till daylight, and although the morning was fortunately cool and breezy during the last three or four miles, the heat was extreme. The next morning we started at half-past three A.M., with the 10th Native Infantry, which had joined us at Bhooj. This regiment (or rather a wing of it) accompanied us during the whole of our subsequent marches; and no words are too strong to express their fidelity before the enemy, their patient endurance of fatigue, and their cheerful readiness to perform their duties, sometimes under most trying circumstances. As we had no longer the benefit of the moon, and the leading squadron was marching nearly five miles an hour, the rear squadron, owing to some slight delay, lost sound of the rest of the column, and we had about two miles of hard trotting across country in total darkness, over ground full of large holes. The next morning our ride was more exciting still; for our guide lost his way, and brought us to a river, which we had to ford. It was so dark that we could not distinguish the ground at all, and we had to ride on, although our horses floundered shoulder-deep into holes, or stepped and scrambled over rocks, every moment. The fourth march brought us to Chowbarree, where we dismissed the beautiful bullocks and handsome carts which had carried our baggage from Bhooj As we hear that the bullocks in the northern and central part of India are mostly a miserable and half-starved race, we have purchased a pair of the magnificent white ones, for which Cutch is famous, to draw our gharry. The country now slightly improves in beauty. At intervals there are trees and patches of cultivation, and we have passed several large tanks, covered with water-fowl. Game continues very abundant; and the wild dogs and jackals prowl at night close to the tents, making the air reverberate with their screaming laugh. Jeesra and Geree, where we encamped in a dry salt marsh, full of tall reeds, which kept us constantly on the watch for fear of fire, Moorania, and Fowar,

were passed before our next halt. Between the
two last we crossed the Runn of Cutch, the eastern
boundary of the Rao's dominions, and entered the
Palampoor States. The Runn is alternately a sandy
and muddy stretch of land, which, during the
monsoon, is covered with salt-water. After crossing
four miles of dry mud, we came to a small sandy
island, called " Gadka Gote," covered with grass and
small bushes. Entering again upon the Runn, we
reached another island, called " Blurdia," of the same
kind as the first. The Runn, which becomes hard
and consistent by December, presents no obstacles,
except in cases of unseasonable rain; and at this
point is about twelve miles across.

After marching through Babra and Warye we
halted again for a day at Radhinpoor, which is a large
and prettily situated native town, surrounded by a
wall. The political agent for the Palampoor States
resides here, as does also the Nawaub, whose gardens
are extensive, and afforded us a shady and agreeable
promenade. We despatched letters to England from
this place *viâ* Deesa, whence ours were forwarded to
us at Warye, dated 4th and 15th January.

On the 25th February we quitted our pleasant
camp at Radhinpoor, and betook ourselves along one
of the dustiest tracks I ever rode, about thirteen
miles to Ooun. The moon lighted us for the first
hour of our March, which began at three A.M.; but
several times, although the night was clear and

bright, I was unable to discern the man riding immediately in front of my horse's nose, owing to the intense dust in which he was enveloped.   It was no
wonder that the eyes felt as if their lids were lined
with sand-paper, or the skin as though rivers of
water would scarcely slake its thirst.   The Nawaub,
by whose orders carts were supplied to the regiments,
is said to make a good thing of the troops who
pass through his States.   The carts which he provided for the baggage transport were charged to
us at the rate of two annas a mile for the
thirteen miles, and as each officer employed two,
and some six, a goodly amount was paid over to
the Nawaub, who, according to report, gives the
unlucky gari-wallahs what he pleases, and keeps the
rest himself.

We marched into Deesa on Sunday morning, the
28th February, at about eight o'clock.   With the
exception of the few days' halt at Bhooj, we had lost
no time upon the road, never marching less than nine
miles, and generally doing from twelve to sixteen
miles a day.   Deesa being the first English station on
our march, we naturally approached it with feelings
of curiosity and excitement; it was, moreover, the
extreme frontier of the quiet districts, and its cantonments once passed, tents can no longer be sent on
overnight, and no messman will be ready to greet us
with tea or coffee on our arrival in camp.   We were
prepared after leaving Deesa to renounce all the

luxuries of the campaign; but we hardly anticipated
the fatigue and discomfort that lay before us.   The
stern schooling of the Crimea had taught us to make
light of difficulties, and although even at this early
stage of the march, we were glad to halt for two or
three days, we nevertheless looked forward to the
future without fear or anxiety.   Deesa is a large,
straggling    cantonment,   with    comfortable-looking
bungalows scattered here and there; but the soil is
so sandy that with the slightest wind the dust becomes
intolerable.   In the native town there are two Parsee
shops, which appear to carry on a thriving trade.
One of these shopkeepers is the agent of our regimental agent in Bombay, and the Mess President
endeavoured in vain to induce him to take charge of
some superfluous stores, so that our baggage was ultimately given over to Government and stowed away
in the barracks.   Our encampment was pitched on a
large plain just outside the cantonment.   We found
here the Queen's 89th, the 17th Native Infantry, a
native cavalry regiment, and Captain Bolton's company of Royal Artillery.

Although we knew that our destination was Kotah,
we were at first in ignorance of the route which we
were to follow.   It was evident that we were to lose
no time upon the road; and in order that we might
save about sixty miles, it was proposed that instead
of going by Nusseerabad, we should take a more
direct track, leading over the Chutterbooj Pass, which

no regular troops had ever crossed before. This
route at first sight appeared totally impracticable for
cavalry, as no stores could be carried on carts, and
as the Commissariat declined to enter into any con-
tract with the natives for the supply of grain and
grass, having no hope of its punctual fulfilment.
Another serious obstacle on this new route was the
apprehended deficiency of water. However, after a
great deal of consultation and consideration, Colonel
De Salis, who commanded the column, resolved on
proceeding by the main road as far as Erinpoora, and
there awaiting final instructions as to whether he
should or should not proceed by the Chutterbooj
Pass. Three hundred pack bullocks were furnished
to the regiment to carry grain from Erinpoora, to be
used in case of the failure of local supplies, and fifty
fresh troop ghorawallahs were also procured to supply
the places of the Sindians who left us at Deesa, the
enormous pay of 15 rupees a month not being a sufficient bribe to induce them to remain. Of course we
had to reduce our baggage to the smallest possible
amount, and we suffered great inconvenience in consequence during the rainy season, having neither
warm clothes nor waterproofs with us. Indeed, I
should probably have lost my life had not an acquaintance, made at a later period, given me the thick
cloth cape of a regimental cloak as some protection
when in my saddle.

At one A.M. on Thursday morning, March the 4th,

we left Deesa, and marched sixteen miles and a half
to Koachawarra. We had crossed two shallow
streams, and passed two villages, when one of our
vicious little troopers struck out at Sergeant Major
Warde, who was riding up the column, and broke
both the bones of his leg below the knee. He continued to ride for three or four minutes without being
aware of the extent of the injury, and was then placed
in a doolie and sent back to Deesa, where there is a
good hospital. We subsequently learned that when
he had recovered from the accident he was sent to re-
gain his strength at the sanatorium on Mount Aboo,
where he was attacked with pneumonia and died.

Being entirely dependent upon camels for the
transport of our baggage, the labour of shifting
camp is immense. For the mess alone, seventy
camels have to be laden. As in many instances they
will not allow a European to approach them, and as
the native servants occupy an interminable time in
arranging the load of each, the packing occupies the
greater part of the night. My husband indented at
Deesa for twelve camels, but after a few marches
sickness overtook them, and we found fifteen requisite to carry our tents, with the servants' baggage
and our own. We expected to be tolerably tired of
marching before reaching Kotah, which at that time
we looked upon as our final destination, and were
already somewhat inclined to agree with the butler
of one of the officers of the 8th Hussars, who begged

to give him warning, for " he found it too much plenty marching."

On Friday, the 5th, we made a thirteen-mile march to Muddar, of which the latter part was as varied and beautiful as the first was monotonous and wearisome. We were now surrounded by rocky eminences, and in sight of the Mount Aboo range of hills. Our camp was pitched for the first time on tolerably hard ground, instead of on the everlasting sand, and we placed our own tent beneath a wide-spreading tamarind tree, the green branches of which afforded a delicious shade.

The next day we pushed on to Reodur, ten miles nearer the beautiful hills. Here we also enjoyed the advantage of a cool and shady camp. H.M.'s 95th Regiment, which preceded us on this march, attacked and took the village of Rowa, about six miles from Reodur. It was occupied by the rebels, a gang of whom, to the number of two hundred, infest these heights, and are the annoyance and terror of all the country side. Secure among the fastnesses of the mountains, they descend like vultures upon the plain. One day they appear on the northern, the next day on the southern side of the hills, and swoop down upon some devoted village, which they sack without mercy.

Major Chetwode went out from this place in quest of a tiger, from the ravages of which the inhabitants had suffered severely; but as the regiment made no halt, he was unable to devote sufficient time to the pursuit. Lieutenant the Hon. E. Stourton, who had been for some days suffering very severely from fever, has experienced so grave a relapse that the medical officers determined on leaving him at the sanatorium, whither he was conveyed from Maira, our next encampment, directly at the foot of Mount Aboo. My recollections of this camp are most pleasant. The mountain, in all its solitary grandeur, rose before us, unmarked by any dwelling or foot-print of man. Now and then the wild cry of a hawk might he heard, as he wheeled high over our heads; and beneath our feet were little star-like flowers and blossoming shrubs. As the shades of evening gathered around us, we walked towards the mountain—tearing our feet with thorns and filling our hands with flowers; nor did we turn back until it was dark, and when we reached the camp it was so late that we had little more than two hours to sleep, before the *reveillée* (that remorseless call) summoned us again to our saddles.

It appears to be General Roberts' intention to wait at Nusseerabad until we can join him. We are certainly hastening towards him with all speed, having marched six days without a halt. The fatigue, however, begins to tell heavily on the three-year-old horses, and also upon the 10th Native Infantry and Captain Bolton's company of Royal Artillery, who accompany us as far as Erimpoora. At length, after

E

six days' marching, came a blessed day of rest at
Serohee. I do not know one of my English acquaintance who can thoroughly appreciate a day of
rest. A halt-day is to us what the Sabbath is to
a man employed in monotonous and toilsome labour
all the week. It seems to me as though when the
halt-day comes I cannot rest enough. Oh! the
inappreciable luxury of a whole clear day, with no
*reveillée* to disturb one at midnight, no camels to
pack, no sleepy horses to rouse up and saddle, no
tents to strike, no dusty march and long-delayed
breakfast, no dinner hurried over that the large tent
may be struck before dusk!

Serohee is a large town, well situated on the side
of a hill. It is famous for its manufacture of swords,
which are of considerable value and beauty.

Letters of the 2nd February were received this
morning. The "Home News," of the same date,
which had arrived three days before, contained a
detailed account of the marriage of the Princess
Royal, and also of the attempt to assassinate the
Emperor of the French. It is quite refreshing to
see that the French army has abandoned all pretence
as to *La Belle Alliance.* As far as individuals were
concerned, it was a humbug throughout. The
national antipathy has not diminished, and the in-
conceivable bombast of the French soldier oozes out
in the pompous addresses to the Emperor.

We have gained one great advantage by entering

the disturbed country, and that is, that the servants and baggage-men, duly impressed with the fear of being cut off, keep up much more closely with the column than heretofore; so that our tents are pitched and breakfast ready almost in time to save me from fainting either from exhaustion or the sun. One of our ghorawallahs has provided himself with a sword; and Lieutenant-Colonel Naylor's servant has procured a bow and arrows, just like the fatal instruments in the tragedy of " Cock Robin." One or two more have armed themselves with boar-spears; and this reminds me that, a day or two before we arrived at Serohee, a wild boar charged through our column when on the line of march. It is well known that a boar will never swerve from his straight course for the purpose of attacking any object: so, as a passage was quickly made for him, he shot through without injuring man or horse.

The Rajah of Serohee visited our camp, and rode through it in state, during the day we halted there. He was escorted by a large armed party, who were at first refused admission into our lines, through a misapprehension, which was rectified almost as soon as it was made.

It was interesting, as our march wore on, to see the various wild animals with which India abounds; for instance, between Serohee and Palree, two bears (these were more strange than pleasant) passed

through our column, on their way from their noc-
turnal wanderings to their den in the mountains.
One or two officers fired revolvers at them, but I
fancy without much effect; had my husband been
riding near, he might have given another proof of
his great accuracy as a pistol-shot. On the day
we reached Erimpoora, graceful little antelopes
came to wonder at us. It was here that we for
the first time came upon traces of this terrible
mutiny. Ruined bungalows and gardens laid waste,
showed how ruthless had been the destroyers. The
Bengalees of the Joudpoor Legion, some of whom
were stationed at Erimpoora when we passed through,
were the instigators and executors of the revolt.
Captain Conolly, who commanded them, and who
was at the time the only European officer residing
at the station, was saved through the connivance
of some of the native officers who remained faithful.
Reports differ as to the manner in which he effected
his escape. I was told that he overheard some of
his men planning his death, and while at his wit's
end to know how to escape, a friendly subadar came
to him and said, " You will find a horse waiting
for you outside the cantonment. Get to him un-
perceived, as best you can, then mount, and I
need not tell you not to spare your spurs." The
last injunction, my informant added, he fulfilled
so well, that he did not check his gallop till
twenty miles lay between him and his would-be

assassins. Now, for the correctness of this I cannot vouch—

> "I know not what the truth may be,
> I tell the tale as 'twas told to me."

Two of this same legion acted as our guides for several days, and a few were not a little suspicious of them. However, they proved faithful and harmless. The detachment of Royal Artillery under Captain Bolton left us to-day, and proceeded to Nusseerabad. It was believed that General Roberts would take with him to Kotah the artillery then at Nusseerabad, and that Captain Bolton's men would supply their places there; but after we had been some days before Kotah, we had the pleasure of falling in with them again. The authorities appear resolved to try the mettle of the horses and the constitutions of the men and officers of H. M.'s 8th Hussars; for, besides giving us a route never passed before by any troops, except when on one occasion five hundred of the Joudpoor Legion scrambled along it, we find that the marches are, in reality, much longer than they are reported to be in the book of the quartermaster-general. Our first march from Erimpoora to Ballee was entered as fourteen miles, but it proved to be seventeen. The next day, to Gomerao was mentioned as fifteen miles; but the infantry were seven hours and five-and-twenty minutes on the line of march, and the cavalry, who started at three A.M., did not reach their camping-ground until fifteen minutes past nine, although they never halted for more than a quarter of an hour at a time. The regiment is supposed to march from three miles and a half to four miles an hour, after the first mile or two, during which they move faster. The luckless ghorawallahs and camp-followers, who were on foot, came in quite useless from fatigue; and our sick men began to increase in number. There were two officers on the sick report, Lieutenant-Colonel Naylor, and Hon. E. Stourton, who was left at Mount Aboo, and of whom no tidings were heard for a long while. The increasing heat of the weather deprives us of nearly all the refreshment of the day's rest. We keep our hearts up, nevertheless, with the hope that when we arrive at Kotah we shall be repaid for the hurry of this march, said, by officers who have previously served in India, to be the most harassing they ever undertook. I do not know whose coughs are the worst, those of the native servants or those of the horses. During the few hours allotted to rest, the noise of coughing horses, choking natives, and remonstrative camels, is enough to banish sleep from every one in camp. As many of the camels are weak and ill-fed, they not unfrequently fall with their loads; and it is no unusual thing to see a bedstead arrive in two or three pieces, a chair minus the seat, or a table wanting a leg. Lucky, indeed, do we consider ourselves if both chairs and table survive the breakfast, without giving way. Here let me remark, for the benefit of others, that the only chairs suited to such an expedition as ours are the portable iron ones manufactured by Messrs. Brown and Sons, of Piccadilly. They fold quite flat, and are easily carried, besides being strong and comfortable. Our bullock gharry, while following the baggage on the line of march from Gomerao to Sommair, was upset into a dry well. It fell completely over, and, strange to say, neither of the bullocks were injured. On its arrival at Sommair, it was taken to pieces, previous to being carried over the Chutterbooj Pass by coolies.

# CHAPTER V.

" All in a hot and copper sky,
    The bloody sun at noon,
Right up above the mast doth stand
    No bigger than the moon."
                            COLERIDGE.

" And sometimes thro' the mirror blue
The Knights came marching two and two."
                            TENNYSON.

ON the morning of the 16th March, the *reveillée*
sounded at three A.M., and shortly before five o'clock
the regiment started, as the day broke, to march
to Jeelwarra.    Lieutenant-Colonel Naylor, whose
gharry, like our own, had been taken to pieces,
started his coolies at midnight with their load, and
mine followed an hour or two later.    The troops
soon found themselves on a rough and rocky path,
leading towards the heart of the mountains.    We
crossed two little hill torrents, and passed at first
under thickly-spreading trees, which diminished in
beauty as we ascended.    I have no doubt that in the
clefts and caves of the rugged hill-sides " many a
fierce she-bear lies amidst bones and blood;" and,
in fact, a bear was seen near the centre of the

column. On and upward we scrambled in single file, over masses of rock and large loose stones; passing with difficulty in one narrow place an unfortunate camel of our advance party, which had laid down to die. Once the road was cut out of the side of the mountain, and we looked down a most uncomfortable depth. It was singular that the Arab horses, so careless when the road is level and smooth, should on this day pass without hesitation or mistake over ground where a false step would have been irrecoverable. A sufficiently hazardous undertaking it was to move troops up so narrow and steep a pass, commanded by a fort, and by eminences from which twenty men might have most seriously annoyed the two regiments. A part of the 10th Native Infantry marched in front, and the remainder of the 10th, with forty of our own men, who were dismounted for the purpose, acted as rear and baggage guards. We marched as quickly as possible through the gorge, occasionally dismounting and leading our horses up the most difficult places. The Pass extended, I believe, from seven to eight miles; and about two miles and a half after we had reached the more open ground at the top, we came to Jeel-warra, most inhospitably situated on a bare and rocky soil; producing, however, one fine banyan-tree, under which we were so fortunate as to be able to pitch our tent.

I felt at this time the first symptoms of over-fatigue and want of sleep, and found that the three, or at most four hours allowed for repose were no longer sufficient to compensate for the fatigues of the day. Satisfied, however, with the report of an easy march for the morrow, I endeavoured to compose myself to sleep. As we were to descend the ghaut, and pass over more rough ground, the *reveillée* did not sound until half-past three; and when parade sounded at about twenty minutes after four, we mounted and groped our perilous way to the front of the column, where we remained until the first streak of dawn, when we commenced the descent. The "good road" proved very like the one of yesterday, except that it was down hill, instead of up. After slipping and scrambling down the rocky paths, we reached the town of Chutterbooj, and came to a rather more sandy and comfortable country. Here we were met by a riding-camel, with a native bearing a note from the officer of our advance party, who had gone on the previous day at noon. The note contained the cheerful intelligence that the road was a very bad one; and that instead of the distance being eleven miles, as stated, it was a good five-and-twenty. By this time the sun was up, and he caught the sides of our faces, which scorched as though blackening beneath his touch. The anxiety that we felt was not so much for ourselves, mounted as we were, but for our unfortunate servants, ghora-wallahs, and camels. Many of the young troop-

horses were also greatly fagged. It appeared to us
that great carelessness had been manifested in the
route chosen, and that the political agent of the
Polampoor States must have been satisfied with very
inaccurate measurements. It is always difficult to
judge of distances in India, as the "kos," or native
mile, differs in different parts of the country.
Sometimes we found a "kos" to signify two English
miles, and sometimes three. On the day of which
I am now writing the men fell into parade at Jeelwarra at a quarter-past four A.M., and they dismounted at the camping-ground at Aimatti at about
twenty minutes past one P.M., while the baggage-
camels did not come up until between five and six
o'clock in the evening. I would not have changed
places with the officer of the rear-guard that day
upon any consideration; as it was, when the halting-
ground was reached, I was obliged to be assisted
from my saddle, being too cramped to dismount
without help. There was no dinner at mess that
night, and our own servants did not arrive until so
late, and were so knocked up when they did, that
it was useless to expect any dinner from them. Had
it not been for the hospitality of the officer who
commanded the advance party, we should have gone
fasting to sleep. The Rajah of Aimatti is related
to the Rajah of Kotah; and his town, when we
were there, was garrisoned by 2,000 men. The
walls look as though they were built of gingerbread-

nuts. No European soldiers were admitted within
them; but our native servants were supplied willingly
enough. The inhabitants have some expert thieves
among them; for they stole two swords and a carbine
from a tent, with securely-fastened doors, in which
eight men were sleeping at the time. We halted
for a day at Aimatti, as well we might; and on the
following morning a march of six miles over a
smooth and level country to Lowa enabled us to
place our camp between a grove of fine tamarind-
trees and a very picturesque, although ruined, fort.
Here we had an opportunity of watching the natives
extracting opium from the fresh and green poppy-
heads, the flowers of which had just fallen. Large
tracts of country are devoted to the cultivation of
this gaudy, but misused plant; and we most impru-
dently stayed in the sun, watching the labourers,
who, with an instrument resembling a three-pronged
fork, were making incisions on each side of
the poppy-head. The morning after this operation,
they return provided with a knife, the blade of
which resembles a small sickle, and on this they
scrape off the dark juice which has oozed through
the incisions. The quantity taken from each head
is so small, that the labour of collecting it is very
tedious. The syrup, when collected on the knife,
resembles a juicy pulp of a dark brown colour. I
should not omit to mention that this day's march,
which we found in the route furnished to Colonel

De Salis to be twelve miles, was barely half the
distance.   May the mistakes in future be always
on this side !   The commissariat arrangements are
now so bad, that sometimes after a severe march
a very insufficient quantity of hay, and only $3\frac{1}{2}$ lbs.
of grain, instead of their allowance of 10 sirrs, or
nearly 12 lbs., are issued for the horses.   Our
private letters from Poonah and Kirkee speak strongly
of the mutinous feeling which smoulders at those
places.   Secret meetings are being held, and great
hopes are excited that the Nana, who is reported
to have slipped his northern moorings, will hasten
down to the vicinity of Poonah, and rally the
Mahrattas to his standard.   Strange scenes, the
effect of panic fears, are said to have been enacted
by the residents at that place, where an elderly
officer, who happened at the time to be quite disabled,
in consequence of a fall from his horse, was in great
request to sleep in the houses of the ladies whose
husbands were absent, by way of guard.

A march of twenty miles (stated to be ten)
brought us the next day to Gangapoor, a town of
some importance as to size.   We encamped near it
in what was evidently the bed of a tank in the rainy
season.   Water was abundant in the neighbourhood,
two large and picturesque lakes, covered with water-
fowl, were on our right hand, and a tank near the
town on our left.   The birds of India are an interesting study.   If their voices are unmusical,—and there

is a proverb in India, that "the birds have no song, the women no beauty, and the flowers no perfume," —the beauty and brilliancy of their plumage far exceeds that of our northern songsters. It is no unusual thing to see fifteen or twenty peacocks at a time. We frequently pass them in the grey morning, roosting on the trees, or coming down in clusters to feed. Then there is the Sáras,* of a French grey and white colour, with red near the bill : this bird is nearly as tall as a man, and often in the morning light appears of gigantic proportions. The white egrets, and paddy-birds, Brahmin kites and hawks, are amongst the larger birds, as well as several others, apparently of the flamingo and bittern tribes, which my ignorance does not enable me to name. Parrots, orioles, jays, mainas,† mango-birds, and others, small but brilliant, dart through the sunshine like flashes of light. Every sort of duck can be shot upon the tanks; and a day or two before we reached this place Major Chetwode killed an alligator which he saw basking on the bank. It moved towards the water directly it perceived him, but having a rifle, he fired instantly: the ball entered behind the shoulder, a second shot was quickly given, but the creature, although mortally wounded, took to the water. None of the beaters cared to go

* A crane, *Grus antigone.*
† The *maina* is a name applied to several birds of the starling family.

in and bring him out. There was no time to lose:
so Major Chetwode, whose promptness and decision
are well known amongst sportsmen, sprang after
him, and dragged him on shore. Although the
creature measured only about eight feet in length,
I looked with wonder into his enormous mouth, the
jaws of which, if roughly closed, sounded as though
made of hard wood.

Gorlam, distant from Gangapoor about fifteen
miles, was the next place where we pitched our
tents. A proof of the dryness of the Indian atmosphere was afforded this morning by the showers of
electric sparks which flew from the tail of the horse
immediately before me. At times the flashes of
light were as strong as those which his iron shoe would
have caused had it come in contact with a flint.
The next day's march brought us to Bheelwarra,
which is surrounded by fine trees and cultivated
ground. To arrive at our encampment we had to
pass through the town, which is handsome and well
built, with broad streets and open squares. Never
before had the inhabitants experienced so great an
excitement. The streets were thronged with spectators,
and the roof of the principal temple was literally
covered with human heads. We observed a long
and low house near the gate by which we made our
exit from the town, the frontage of which was richly
carved and painted; while the massive doors were
fastened by bright steel chains. This proved to be

the bank wherein, during the stay of the gallant 8th Hussars before their walls, the careful inhabitants locked up their women. I was shown a handful of small change from this repository of treasure, of which a cowry, or small shell, formed the most valuable ingredient. I afterwards saw a quantity of these cowries stored up in the strong closet of a merchant's house at Kotah. There are here two large wells or tanks of great depth, one in the centre of the town and the other outside the gate. They are surrounded with ornamental walls and are approached by flights of steps descending beneath archways of stone, supported on light and well-proportioned pillars. During our halt of one day at Bheelwarra we heard of General Roberts being actually before Kotah. We were most unwilling to believe that he had advanced without waiting for us, who have been making such efforts to join him. We still hope that the information is premature; but our uncertainty will cease on our arrival at Jehazpoor, four marches from hence, where Colonel De Salis will receive a communication from the General commanding the division.

Three days before our arrival at Bheelwarra we buried the first man who died during our march. He had long suffered from depression of spirits—a sure forerunner of disease in this climate—and died of dysentery while being carried on the line of march. Our hospitals are now filling, nor can we wonder at it, as so many of our men have to undergo the unusual exertion and exposure to the sun consequent upon attending to their own horses, a thing forbidden in this country, where it is customary for all European regiments to have native grooms. In one troop of the 8th Hussars at this time there are but five ghorawallahs, the rest having absconded soon after leaving Deesa; at which place they were hired, and where they mostly received wages in advance. Our soldiers are thus much exposed, especially in having to transport large sacks of grain from the commissariat to the troop lines.

On the second day's march from Bheelwarra, we reached at sunrise a wide plain with a cluster of trees which sheltered a large tank. Behind them rose the walls of a palace which, at a distance, appeared beautiful and fairy-like enough, to gratify the ideas usually entertained by those who have never seen them of the architectural beauties of eastern buildings. This turned out to be the residence of the Rajah of Shahpoora, who, soon after our arrival, came with several elephants, and an escort of mounted men, to inspect our camp. Later in the day, when we proposed visiting the building which had caused us so much admiration in the morning, we were told by an officer returning from it, that it was a mere ruin of paint, and plaster, and dirt. And yet India can boast of one building, the purity and beauty of which is as transcendent as it

F

is wonderful and glorious. I allude to the gorgeous tomb at Agra, erected by the Emperor Shah Jehan to his wife. Although fallen from its original splendour, it is still a marvel; and Government allots a certain sum to save it from decay. But its gates, which like those of the shrine in the church of St. John at Malta, were of pure silver, have long ago been coined into rupees. Tradition also tells of a door formed of agate, which exists no longer. The tomb itself is of white marble, and the Emperor is said to have planned the erection of a similar resting-place for himself close by, connected with it by a span of white marble.

It was reported in our camp, as we marched next morning, that the Rajah of Shahpoora had sent a thousand armed men to join the force before Kotah. The warriors whom we saw on the previous evening carried matchlocks and round shields made of thick leather. A party of them, accompanied by three elephants and a concourse of followers, came into camp before sunset, and amused us by a display of horsemanship. They described circles and figures when at a galop; they rushed forward at full speed, and then checked their horses suddenly and stood still. The process as practised in India is a cruel one. The bit is so exceedingly severe that it is not unusual to see the horses' mouths streaming with blood. After all said and done, there is no horse-man in the world to be compared to an Englishman

who knows how to ride, plainly and neatly turned
out on a hunting morning, and mounted upon a
handsome thoroughbred English or Irish horse.

The native Indian, the Turk, and the Arab carry
all their bed and household appendages upon their
horse's back, so that the animal, to our notion, is
loaded before he is mounted by his rider, whose seat,
owing to the width of the accumulated loadings, is
very ungainly. The fashion, too, of confining the
horse's head close to his chest, by a tight band or
martingale, deprives him of all freedom or grace of
motion, and causes him to be covered with sweat and
foam.

This neighbourhood, and also that of Jehazpoor,
is rich in garnets, and at the latter place they can be
procured, ready polished, for a mere trifle. Camp
gossip becomes rife as we near Kotah, and it is now
asserted that the town is defended by 22,000 rebels.
The guides on our next march performed their task
very unwillingly, and ours twice asserted that he had
lost his way. That of the 10th Native Infantry lost
his so completely that the regiment did not arrive in
camp until two hours after we had pitched our tents.
The consequence was, that many baggage camels
went astray. As soon as the 10th reached the
ground, they gave their guide a couple of dozen
lashes. A dozen was also administered to one of
our troop cooks, whose habit of loitering on the
march delayed the men's breakfasts an unwarrant-

able time. I hear that he took it with perfect philosophy, and when released, laid down, and slept the remainder of the day; but the next morning the breakfasts of the E Troop were ready before the rest.

On the 26th March, for the first time, we felt the hot winds. They blew like blasts from a furnace, inducing a thirst that nothing could allay. One officer, complaining of this, said, "I drink twenty-five hours out of the twenty-four, and yet cannot quench my thirst."

Mr. Russell, *The Times* correspondent, writing a short time later, thus describes his sensations, which I quote, as entirely resembling my own:—"The hot winds, which set in about ten o'clock, are all but intolerable, charged as they are with dust, which fills every pore and fires the blood—which seems to penetrate the internal mechanism of the body, as it does, in reality, force its way into the works of a watch—which renders all out-of-door exercise a sort of severe penitential infliction, and makes dwelling in tents utterly miserable and hopeless . . . . To the increasing heat," he goes on to say, "will be added length of days, greater power of the wind, and, if possible, more dust. Of the latter it is quite beyond the power of description to give an idea. It is so fine and subtle, that long after the causes which have raised it have ceased to exert their influence, you may see it, like a veil of gauze between you and every object. When this dust is set in motion by the hot wind, and when the grosser sand, composed of minute fragments of talc, scales of mica, and earth, is impelled in quick successive waves, through the heated atmosphere, the effect is quite sufficient to make one detest India for ever."

The regimental orders of this day contain a notification that on our arrival at Jehazpoor a communication will be received from General Roberts, which will probably hurry us as much as possible to the front. We are therefore ordered to hold ourselves in readiness for forced marches. A ride of five-and-twenty or thirty miles at night does not appear formidable, after our march till after "the deep midnoon" from Jeelwarra to Amatti. The next day, according to expectation, the communicacation came. It enclosed a route containing six marches to Kotah, and gave no directions as to the time in which they were to be performed.

# CHAPTER VI.

"BARDOLPH.—On, on, on, on! to the breach, to the breach!
"NYM.—I pray thee, Corporal, stay; the knocks are too hard:
and, for my own part, I have not a case of lives; the humours of
it is too hot, that is the very plain song of it.
"PIST.—The plain song is most just: for humours do abound;
        Knocks go and come: God's vassals drop and die;
            And sword and shield
            In bloody field
            Doth win immortal fame.
"BOY.—Would I were in an ale-house in London! I would give
all my fame for a pot of ale, and safety!"
SHAKSPEARE.

AFTER a march of fourteen miles, we had set up our
camp for the day at Thanna, when, looking out of
our tent, we descried a riding camel with a very gay
saddle, and we knew that despatches had come in.
Overcome with heat and fatigue, I soon after fell
asleep in my chair, when an orderly awoke me, and
said that the Colonel had received a despatch to
hasten the regiment to the front, and that we
were to march, at eight P.M., twenty-two miles, to
Boondee. Officers were so far fortunate that they
could have a change of horses, and the troopers,
when they started, were wonderfully fresh. The
country through which we passed must have been

lovely, although we could not see it. Our road defiled through mountain passes, with a gate and fortification erected on the summit. Thence we descended until we reached a fertile valley, and a river, wherein the horses were watered; soon after we passed the lake, above which frown the walls and towers of Boondee, and by half-past three A.M. had reached our halting-place on the far side of the town. Several hundred Bengalee sepoys were reported to be in this place, the fortifications of which, natural and otherwise, appeared of immense strength. The inhabitants manifested an unwillingness to supply our advance party, which preceded us by a few hours, but brought provisions readily enough to us. On our arrival, at half-past three A.M., very few tents were pitched, as we only rested until the horses and camels were refreshed. I was indebted to the great kindness of the officer in command of the advance party, who, directly I arrived, insisted on giving up his tent for my use. Thick groves of mango, pomegranate, tamarind, and palm trees, formed a screen from the sun, which rendered a tent less necessary. "Boots and saddles" sounded at two o'clock, and by three P.M. we were again on the line of march. The sun blazed down upon the white and dusty road, but every hour decreased his fierceness, a fortunate thing for us, as one-and-twenty miles still lay between us and Kotah. It was about half-past eleven P.M. when we first discerned in the distance the lights of the

camp. About a mile from our encamping ground
two men of the 1st Bombay Lancers, whose admirable conduct at Nusseerabad, when they escorted
all the Europeans to places of safety, is worthy of
the greatest praise, met us and showed us the position
we were to take up. Looking at my watch by the
moonlight on arriving in camp, I found it was five-
and-twenty minutes to two A.M.

During the four last miles we had heard the guns
firing on the town; but our astonishment was great,
on our arrival, to see Colonel De Salis reading brigade
orders before the men had dismounted, to the effect
that an assault was to be made at noon, and that the
cavalry, 8th Hussars included, would turn out at
seven A.M., prepared to take their share in the action!

This was sharp work " and no mistake." And I
must say that I observed with pleasure and with
pride, that after two months' wearisome marching,
after fifty-six hours of great exertion, with tired
horses for which not a draught of water could be
procured, without rest, or refreshment for themselves,
save what the bare earth afforded, there were none
who did not show that eager excitement and cheerful
readiness which never seem to desert the English
soldier in the field. By half-past seven the cavalry
brigade marched off the ground, 1,500 strong, and
apparently as fine a body of men as one would wish
to see. There were 8th Hussars, and Bombay
Lancers, Jacob's Sind Horse, some Belooches on their

little ragged tattoos, and Lieutenant-Colonel Blake's troop of Bombay Horse Artillery.

We, who were thankful enough for some few hours' rest from our saddles, whence

"We had oft outwatched the Bear,"

and the 150 men left to guard the standing camp, waited with a thirsty anxiety for news. The firing on the town struck us, who were accustomed to the rain of shot at Sebastopol, as remarkably slack—far too much so to justify the information we received last night, which was, that the town was to be bombarded from daybreak until about ten o'clock, when the infantry were to force their way into the place by the Rajah's gate, and the cavalry having crossed the river by a ford about seven miles up, in order to reach the only open side of the town, were to intercept and destroy the rebels should they attempt to escape. As we were not then aware that the greater part of the garrison had already fled, the plan appeared an admirable one. In theory it was perfect—in practice, however, it turned out the reverse.

At two o'clock a rattle of musketry, which continued for about five minutes, made us order the least weary of our horses, and start in the direction of Kotah, distant about a mile and a half. Nothing occurred to interrupt us, and we rode on without any incident beyond the astonishment caused by the apparition of a lady in camp to a native infantry officer, who involuntarily checked his horse and continued staring until we were nearly out of sight. We soon gained an eminence overlooking the river and the Rajah's palace, together with the gate by which our troops had already entered the town. Just as we reached this spot a great explosion took place, fatal, as we afterwards learnt, to several men of the 95th Regiment. Some foot soldiers and several of the Sind Horse were visible near the gate, and the noise made by human voices inside the walls was perfectly incredible; it was like an enormous beehive. The heat of the sun was intense; and as we could see nothing besides the fortifications, and could gain no information, we returned to our tent. We heard the next day that while we were watching the town, between two and three P.M., the remainder of the mutineers were escaping from the opposite gate. They evacuated the town in haste, but without disorder, passing quickly over the plain until they reached a few houses known as " The Rebels' Village," where they formed for their march.

It will naturally be asked—" Where were the 1,500 cavalry and artillery at this time, and what were they doing towards the destruction of the flying enemy ?" The cavalry and artillery reached the ford at the appointed time, and had traversed half its width, in spite of the difficulties which it presented, when some one with keener eyes than the rest discovered what he declared to be a gun pointed on the wading force. On nearer and careful examination, it proved to be a black buffalo grazing. At last, after a good deal of delay, and some little disorder, the ford was crossed. I hesitate to describe what followed. The cavalry and artillery were immediately halted on the river bank, and the men remained standing to their horses or lying under the trees until two o'clock, when the enemy, unable to endure the fierce assault of the infantry, fled across the plain, carrying with them their arms, ammunition, and treasure! Surely on receipt of this intelligence, the cavalry must have started in hot pursuit. No. Far from it. *They remained where they halted all that day and all that night; and the next morning they marched into Kotah, and then returned to their original halting-place by the ford!*

Greatly disheartened and humiliated did both officers and men feel at this ignominious termination of their gallant efforts to get up in time to take part in the siege. They were forced into this false position without any obvious reason, and at a time when a fair opportunity offered of adding fresh honour to their Crimean name. On the evening of the next day an order was sent to our camp desiring us to join the regiment at the ford. So we struck our tents and mounted our horses, starting a little before ten. It was fortunate for us that the moon was up and near the full, for after marching about seven miles we came to the broad, broad river; it did not reach

our horses' girths, but its bed was filled with masses
of rock and large boulders. Slowly the horses crept
across, now plunging up to their shoulders as they slid
off a boulder, now poising themselves on a rock
which rose above the surface. The white Arab
which my husband rode shivered and snorted at
every step, but " Prince," who carried me, was calm
and brave, and only lost his footing once or twice.
We crossed far more easily than did the main body
of the regiment the day before, when, as I am told,
many horses were down. It was one o'clock when
we reached the camp, and we found all the officers
astir, for the flying column which was to go in
pursuit of the escaped rebels was being organized,
and the orders then just issued were for two squadrons
to join detachments of other cavalry regiments and
artillery, and to start at daybreak. A harassing
night to men and officers resulted. Orders and
counter-orders, a delayed commissariat, and other
reasons, prevented the one squadron, which eventually
went under the command of Major Chetwode, from
marching until four P.M. It was hard upon the men
to arouse them at midnight for a service upon which
they were not required to start until sixteen hours
afterwards! And had the brigade been otherwise
commanded there would have been no necessity for a
pursuit at all, for few Acting Brigadiers would have
halted their men for twenty-four hours with a flying
enemy almost in sight. The fugitives, who had

gained fifty-two hours' start, were now to be pursued by our troopers in full marching order and on jaded horses!

The 95th, 10th Native Infantry, and the artillery, with their doolies, camels, gharrys, grass-cutters and camp-followers, marched by our tent-door before eight o'clock. Amongst the camp-followers was a handsome clumber spaniel which had lost sight of his master. He came for a moment to the shade of my tent, and then left it in search of his owner. I fetched a gindy full of fresh water, and had it waiting for him, for I felt sure I should see his foolish, honest face again, and after about half an hour back he came. Poor thirsty dog! How he panted and lapped, and then laid down close to the water, and made himself quite at home till evening, when he wagged his tail to me, and wandered forth again. It is a mistaken feeling of affection which brings English dogs into this fierce climate. They suffer cruelly, and are rarely long-lived. Even " Jim," the dog of many fights, who has been with the 8th Hussars ever since they landed in Bulgaria in 1854, who went through the Danubian expedition, and was present at Alma and Balaklava, and was wounded at Inkermann—who wore a Crimean medal for twelve months at Dundalk, and accompanied the regiment on its voyage to Bombay, and on its march to Kotah—even he, although " held up bravely by the brave heart within," begins to show the effects of heat and thirst. When leg-weary on the march, he will fall back until he recognises one of his particular friends amongst the men, when he puts his fore-paws on the stirrup-iron, and gets a ride on the front of the saddle. Great will be the grief, universal the mourning, whenever death claims " Jim :" and sturdy and quick is the vengeance wreaked upon man or dog who presumes to molest this regimental favourite.

On the afternoon of the 1st April, an explosion took place in the town of Kotah, which was distinctly visible in our camp. A quantity of the enemy's powder, which had been parked, previously to being transported to our lines, had been left under a native guard. Some disaffected persons in the town ignited it, and several men and two officers of the 95th were killed and others wounded by the explosion. A havildar and two men, forming part of the guard, who happened to be in a shed inside the yard where the powder was, were blown to atoms. Two native sentries outside the wall never moved from their posts. They stood firm, although to have done so must have appeared to them certain and instant death. Strange to say, neither of them was hurt. They were especially recommended to General Roberts commanding the division.

An arbitrary abuse of power has for some time caused great annoyance and discontent throughout our regimental camp. No officer is permitted to

purchase forage for his horses, nor even to leave
the camp, until the commissariat officer has supplied
the proper amount of forage to the troop-horses.  In
India every officer buys forage for his own horses at
his own cost, independently of the commissariat; and
now, if he purchases hay, even at a distant village,
it is taken from him in case the troopers, through
the neglect of the commissariat, have not received
a full supply.  To visit the failures of the commissariat upon every officer in the regiment, seems
to me both unjust and unwarrantable; and I write
feelingly, as in consequence of not being permitted
to purchase what is freely offered for sale, our beautiful white bullocks have had no grass for two days.
Of course our horses, and I believe those of every
officer in the regiment were equally deprived of their
grass.

At the end of this our most unsatisfactory first
act, we are told that our destination is either
Neemuch or Nusseerabad.  We have heard to-day,
April 8th, that the rebels, having got away from
Lucknow, are making for Central India.  It is
thought that the delay of Sir Hugh Rose's column
at Saugor has afforded them the opportunity of going
southwards.  It is easy to foresee that this will give
us employment; so we no longer reckon with delight
and certainty upon the bungalows of Neemuch.  Indeed, it appears that so long as we remain in what our
Bandmaster Herr Adolphe König energetically calls

" this detestable country," we must always be engaged
either in flight from, or in pursuit of an enemy.
The foe that especially annoys us now is numerous,
and always acting on the offensive — harassing us
night and day; destroying, not only our comfort,
but our clothes. It is none other than that scourge
of India, the white ant. It is impossible for any
one who has not resided in the country to form an
idea of the depredations committed by these destruc-
tive little insects. Wooden boxes, carpets, leathern
bags, straps, saddles, linen, bridles, boots, tent and
tent-pole, are all equally the objects of their rapacity.
Nothing excludes them but glass or tin, and camphor
wood, which they cannot endure. So secret and
so speedy are they, that it is no unusual thing to
see the soles of boots, which have lain by for only
one day, half eaten through. Fortunately nearly
all our boxes are lined with tin; and we have taken
the additional precaution of raising them from the
ground on bottles. Carpets, &c., require looking
to, at least twice a day; and it is a good plan to
put all small leathern articles on tables, the legs of
which stand in iron saucers filled with water.

An instance of antique heroism, uncommon in
these civilized days, occurred during the assault on
Kotah. The rebel chiefs were endeavouring to
make the most favourable disposition of their forces,
and one of them rode with considerable difficulty
to the top of a fortification, from whence he could

command a view of all that was going on. As the
mutineers began to fly, and the English pressed
into the town, it became evident to him that, before
he could descend, the enemy would be upon him,
and escape would be impossible. Choosing death,
rather than the disgrace of falling alive into our
hands, he gathered up his reins, and plunging his
armed heels into his horse's sides, rode him at the
parapet-wall. The horse rose bravely at his last
leap, and falling headlong with his rider a depth of
120 feet, both were crushed in one mangled mass
together. In the days of Saladin and *Cœur de Lion*,
that corpse would have been carefully gathered up,
and reverently buried, instead of being left to be
devoured by the pariah dogs and pigs.

We have at last received news of our flying
column, which has been out for eleven days. A
despatch has come in, saying that although they have
been unable to come up with the main body of the
rebels, yet they have taken seven guns, and are now
waiting for orders. The squadron of the 8th Hussars
reports only one man sick, and only four horses with
sore backs—wonderfully less than we anticipated.

On the first afternoon that there was a slight breeze,
we started on horseback, a party of four, to ride into
Kotah, and see as much as we could of the town.
We passed the camps of the 10th Native Infantry and
Her Majesty's 95th, and shortly after came upon the
ruins of the bungalows that had been destroyed. The

principal of these was the Residency, where Major
Burton had lived, whose murder the rebels have now
such deep cause to regret; and near it is the burial-
ground, where his daughter lies buried underneath a
handsome tomb.    The houses, pleasantly situated
amidst large trees and flowering shrubs, presented
mere shells, and all things around told the same tale
of desolation.   A large ornamental well, with broken
trough, stood in one of the enclosures; but the only
beings at home amongst the general ruin were the
monkeys, which played among the trees, and sprang
from branch to branch, as gaily as though no human
blood had ever stained the soil beneath them.    The
fortifications which surround the town of Kotah are
wonderfully massive.   We read in the Bible of persons inhabiting houses built in the thickness of the
wall at Jericho, but these walls are so thick that there
is a deep moat between the outer gate and that which
opens into the town.    The streets were so strewn
with plunder, that our horses positively walked over
cushions, garments, bedsteads, sofas, and Persian
MSS.   We had difficulty to induce them to follow
such a gaudy path, and they proceeded with many
snorts and shies until they gained a clearer thorough-
fare.   A few wailing old men and women were alone
left to mourn for the city; and starving dogs and
bullocks roamed about—gaunt, hungry, and grim.
We went into some of the temples, but found
nothing of interest.   The streets are narrow and ill-

paved, and the town was pervaded by that strong and
pungent smell peculiar to the whole of the East.  As
we were riding out of the town, we met with an
enormous boar which had come in, scenting future
feasts on " all uncleanness."  His tusk gleamed by
his dusky upper lip, and when he saw us he gave a
grunt and began to increase his speed.  Fortunately
we were riding in single file, and he passed me and
Lieutenant Hayes, who rode next, without notice;
but seeing more horses than he liked, he made a dart
at " The Rajah," who avoided him by springing up
a side street.  He then charged the last horse of our
party.  The ill-paved street was so slippery that I
feared the horse must lose his footing; he did not
slip, however, but wheeled sharp round, and darted
off at a rate which showed that he appreciated the
tushes of his foe.

The native servants are possessed by the love of
plunder in an unconquerable degree.  A provost-
sergeant was stationed at the gate nearest camp to
search all out-comers, whom, in case of resistance,
he had power to flog.  Several camel-drivers eluded
him by concealing plundered articles in the hay with
which the camels were laden; but a ghorawallah,
who accompanied his master into the town, endeavoured to cheat " Cerberus " by tying various articles
round his waist, underneath his clothes.  " Hullo ! "
barked Cerberus, " you looks fatter than you did
when you followed your master into the town.

Iderow (come here), you ghorawallah!" And the poor
fellow, as he was unwound, bid

"Farewell, a long farewell to all his greatness,"

with a sorrowful and disgusted face.

Having made ourselves acquainted with the interior
of the town, we organized another party to inspect
the outside of the fortifications.   To gain those on
the eastern side (the one from which the rebels had
escaped), we passed through spacious and shady
gardens, and came upon a group of twenty or thirty
tombs, some of them elaborately carved and adorned
with rich fretwork.   Each of these temple-tombs
was approached by handsome flights of steps, ornamented with carved horses and elephants in bold
relief, while colossal elephants guarded the sacred
portals.   Large trees added to the beautiful effect of
this secluded spot, after passing which we came to
the deep, wide lake, in itself a fortification.   As we
neared the massive walls, flanked by towers and
bastions, with buttress and moat, we saw revolting
evidence of the work of death.   The dogs and pigs
were busy at their work, and it was frightful to see
them tearing at the limbs of the dead.   Near one of
the towers lay two men and three horses; the latter
had their legs hobbled and tied together, as though
the slings had broken in an attempt to lower them
from the top of the tower.   At the foot of another
tower lay the man who had been seen to leap over.

We scared away the unwilling dogs; and I could not help noticing, that where men and horses lay together, the men were devoured before the horses were touched. We returned home through the gardens (needing the fragrance of the flowers), and watered our horses at an irrigated rose-bed.

About this time the inhabitants were permitted to return to the town, which, after many conferences, had been given back to the Rajah—an arrangement which disappointed the hopes of those who were calculating on a large amount of prize-money. At first it was reported that ten pounds weight of jewels had been seized, and that captains would receive at least 400*l.* and subalterns 200*l.*, but these golden visions soon faded away. However, as by general orders of April 7th a return of fighting men and enlisted camp followers was to be sent into head-quarters, it is probable that the rebels left behind them a sufficient sum for every man to receive a share.

I have been over the Residency to-day, and have seen the floor of the supper-room all smeared with blood. It appears that Major Burton's head clerk, Lalla, had conceived a spite against him, and seeing the rebellion ripening he suddenly attacked the Residency with 1,500 men and two guns. Major Burton and his two sons retreated to an upper room, and prepared to defend themselves in spite of the odds of 1,500 against three, and of the round shot

from the guns in the garden, which burst every
moment through the walls.   The river runs by the
back of the Residency; and the old man vainly
entreated his sons, who were expert swimmers, to
leave him and to save their lives.   Firing from the
verandah on each side of their father, for three hours,
they kept the 1,500 men at bay, expecting that the
Rajah of Kotah would send boats down the river to
their father's relief.   The traitorous Rajah sent no
boats; and at last they were wearied out and over-
powered by numbers.   The blood-stains are still
visible on the floor where they fell, and across which
they were dragged, that their bodies might be flung
over to the populace below.

On the 9th April the force before Kotah began to
disperse.  The left wing of the 8th, under Lieutenant-
Colonel Naylor, marched for Nusseerabad, expecting
to go into cantonments there; and on the 16th the
detachment of Sind Horse also left us, having before
them a playful little march of 1,200 miles to
Jacobabad.

# CHAPTER VII.

"Trait'rous knaves, with plots designing,
Trembled at our sheathless sword,
Knowing that its splendrous shining
Was the glory of the Lord."

"The sunbeams are my shafts, with which I kill."
SHELLEY.

"I have lived my life, and that which I have done
May He himself make pure! But thou,
If thou shouldst never see my face again,
Pray for my soul."
*Morte d'Artur.*

THE flying column returned on the morning of the
eleventh of April, bringing with them the captured
guns, and a considerable quantity of ammunition.
They had pursued the flying foe as rapidly as possible, obtaining as they went very little information,
and that little, vague and unsatisfactory. Once they
heard that the main body of the rebels was sixty
miles ahead, and it was debated whether the cavalry
should push on the whole distance at once, but this
plan was wisely rejected; for, independent of the
fatigue, the exposure of Europeans to the sun must
have been attended with fatal consequences. When
they had penetrated as far as the borders of Gwalior,

they learnt that the fugitives, whose track was marked by the bodies of slaughtered men and women, had buried their treasure and dispersed. During their flight a number of sowars always preceded the rebel force, and pressed all the carts and bullocks of the villages, and any attempt at opposition was answered by death. By these means their march was never hindered for want of transport. The exhausted horses, or bullocks, were unharnessed and turned adrift, while pressed ones took their places. So great was their haste, that if a cart broke down it was pushed aside out of the road and left. At one village the atrocities they committed were so outrageous, that the inhabitants, in desperation, rushed out to attack them under cover of the night, crying, " The English are coming! the English are coming !" The effect of this war-cry was magical. Like the Syrians of old " they arose and fled," leaving their camp as it was. The seven guns thus abandoned fell into the hands of the pursuers, who were in reality nearer at hand than the brave villagers had supposed. Some distance further on an eighth gun was discovered among some bushes. We rode up the next day to inspect the guns, which are of brass. One is a small camel gun ; and the rest, although possessing great weight of metal, will only carry a shot of about five and a half or six pounds.

I mentioned before, that amongst the cavalry at

Kotah, there were detachments of Jacob's Sind
Horse, and also of Belooches. The former, judging
by those we saw, must be a very fine body of men.
No married man is enlisted into the corps, or permitted to remain in it; and the anxiety of the Sindians to be admitted into it is said to be very great.
The candidates, if satisfactory in other respects, are
mounted on horseback, without a saddle, and with
a plain watering-bridle. They are then taken to a
steeple-chase ground, extending over two miles, and
supplied, artificially and naturally, with every kind
of obstacle, and told that the first men in will be
chosen. Even before I had heard of this initiatory
process, I used to admire these dashing riders, who
sat so easily on their horses, and looked so well.
During the expedition of our flying column there
was a ford to be crossed—deep, wide, and difficult;
but they made no check. Plunging into it, they
splashed and scrambled through it in ten minutes;
while it took our people, with their steadier notions,
twice that time to cross. They are allowed a certain
sum, out of which they provide their own horses, or
Government perhaps would hardly approve of such
expeditious movements.

The Belooches are a kind of Indian Bashi-Basouks.
They wear their own dress, ride their own tattoos
(little native ponies), and are the most inveterate
plunderers. On entering a village they disperse and
scramble over the roofs, or in at the windows; any-

how, or anywhere, so long as anything in the shape of booty is to be obtained. On one occasion, a native of one of the large villages came, with clasped hands, to prefer a complaint. " They have robbed me and my wife of everything that we possess ; we are stripped, and utterly ruined." The accused were searched, in spite of profuse protestations of inno- cence, but nothing was found. At last suspicion was directed to a saddle; it was taken from the horse's back, and when the lining was ripped open, the stuffing was found to be composed of shawls, scarfs, turbans, and money. " Yes," said the plun- dered victim, " these are mine; but these are not all, there are yet more shawls." The ingenuity of the searchers was at fault, until somebody bethought them of the nose-bags of the horses. There was grain in each; but when the bags were turned upside down, with the grain fell out the missing property. The officer commanding the Belooches having been requested to punish the guilty men severely, as a warning to the rest, soon after sent to say that their horses would be sold and the price put into the prize fund, that they were to receive fifty lashes, to march on foot, and to be imprisoned for six months ; at the same time he requested to know whether these punishments were considered sufficient, or whether he should add anything else.

The irregular cavalry rarely unsaddle their horses, lest by doing so they should disclose the fearful sores upon their backs. So long as their horses will feed, they do not trouble themselves about anything else; but they are careful to provide them with sufficient forage, knowing that without it the little creatures could never perform the work expected of them.

The news of the fall of Jhansi, which reached us yesterday, is confirmed by Colonel Price, commanding the Royal Artillery here.

The head-quarter wing of the 8th Hussars, on leaving Kotah, was to march into cantonments for the hot and rainy seasons at Nusseerabad; but as Colonel De Salis had taken a house at Neemuch, he exerted all his influnce, and eventually with success, to have the head-quarters ordered to Neemuch. Courts-martial on our prisoners have been busy for some time; and on the 13th April sentence was passed upon Kedra Bux, and Alem Gha. The former was acquitted, and the latter sentenced to transportation for life, for aiding and abetting in rebellion against the Government of the East India Company. Several men have been hanged; but as these executions took place, happily for us, on the other side of the river, they did not create interest or disturbance in our camp.

The sun in this perfectly unsheltered plain grows more and more intolerable every day; and living as we do, surrounded by camels, horses, bullocks, and dogs, within a dozen yards of our tent, a standing camp soon becomes unhealthy. The thermometer in

our large tent, at noon, is either 108° or 109°, and in
the baychuba (a single-roofed tent) one degree higher.
The sun blazes and blisters, and " being a God,
kissing carrion," corrupts everything exposed to his
fierce heat. I now feel the effects of our severe
march. My strength is gone. I am unequal to
any effort or fatigue, and look with absolute dread
upon the horses, knowing that I shall soon be compelled to ride them, however unfit I may be. My
mind—overwrought and exhausted—fell back during
my illness to places long ago left, and to friends
many years dead. I fancied myself a child, once
more at home. I could not account for my prolonged
absence, nor why mamma had not sent the carriage
to fetch me—that mother whom I last saw in my
golden childhood laid out in her coffin just twenty
years ago. It is satisfactory to know that our bandmaster, Herr Adolphe König, has reached Bombay,
as the want of his delicious harmony has been felt
and acknowledged by most of us. The band instruments, however, are all in store at Deesa, as they
were found to have been injured by frequent falls
from the backs of unsteady camels.

We left Kotah on the 19th of April, and recommenced our wanderings. General Roberts, with a
party of his division, preceded us by one night on
the road to Neemuch; whither, as we believed, we
were all bound. Brigadier Smith, who had been
detained on his march from Bombay, had lately

joined General Roberts, and taken the command of
his brigade. We started in the expectation of
making an eighteen days' march to Neemuch, with
the prospect of settling in cantonments either there
or at Nusseerabad. It was well we left Kotah when
we did, for it is supposed to be one of the hottest
and most unhealthy places in this part of India.
It becomes of great importance to us to know our
destination before the rains, as in consequence of
having left our mess-stores at Deesa, we are quite
out of supplies. No sherry, no beer—although,
indeed, both are procurable in small quantities from
Parsee rapacity—at four guineas and two guineas a
dozen respectively. Our first march of eleven miles,
to Jugpoora, was accomplished without incident or
adventure. We passed the fragrant trees that
shadow the gardens on the eastern side of Kotah,
and then emerged upon a rocky plain, which must
have given the staunch little horses of the artillery
rough and slippery work. Our halting-place was
near a grove of palm and mango-trees, which shelters
a spring and stream of clearest water. The next
day's march, of eight miles, brought us to Hunoubra,
and here we were nearly having an adventure.
The camel-drivers, after each day's march, take
their camels to graze in the vicinity of the camp;
and it appeared that some camel-drivers of General
Roberts' force, which had passed through Hunoubra
on the previous day, had torn down branches from

the mango-trees to feed their beasts.  The villagers
sought to indemnify themselves by seizing two of our
own private camel-men, whom they beat severely,
robbed, and finally sent back to camp without their
camels.  They came to us immediately to complain,
and the matter was reported to the Brigadier; upon
which, some European soldiers, with an interpreter,
were despatched with orders to bring in the culprits
and the head man of the village.  They came,
escorted by the Hussars, and looking in a terrible
fright.  The punishment, however, was merely an
order to refund the stolen money (ten rupees), and
the administration of a few blows to the head man,
to remind him that it was his duty to keep order.
It was thought that more notice should have been
taken of the matter; for the bungalow, formerly
occupied by the sergeant employed to survey the
roads, had been reduced by the inhabitants to a heap
of ruins; and they were reported to have cut the
throats of two camel-men, who passed through on
a previous occasion with a European force.

Last night, during our long and rough march to
Ahmedpoora, my husband's horse became alarmed;
and, springing aside, lost his footing, and rolled over
a steep embankment.  Fortunately, neither were
hurt, beyond a few cuts and bruises; but when
the white horse galloped wildly away across the
boundless plain in the dim twilight, I never expected
to see him any more.

The villagers scowl at us as we pass. We are
now in the territory through which Holkar chased
General Munsen after having defeated him near the
Mukundra Pass. The roads are infamous. Surely
the Government of India might oblige the various
rajahs to make passable roads through their several
districts. It would very much facilitate the passage
of troops, if it were productive of no other good;
and would entail but a small tax upon each state.
The Rao of Cutch has made a really fine road,
elevated and drained, with bridges, and in places a
footpath, extending from Mandavee to Bhooj, merely
on the suggestion of the Political Agent; whereas
we often marched over very bad and rough tracks,
which, with a little trouble and labour, might have
been level and sound. In going up the Mukundra
Pass, we rode over rocky ways that for a couple
of miles were all but impracticable for guns. Large
masses of rock impeded us at every step, while at
one time we descended a path resembling steep and
uncomfortably narrow stairs, which thirty or forty
men, with hammers and blasting-powder, might in
a few weeks have converted into a good road.
Bridges might be constructed by the same means
over the many rivers, which are impassable during
the rains; and which, even in the dry season, present
deep, rocky, and dangerous fords. On the trunk-
road, near Mahona, it was a real pleasure to see a
beautiful and well-built bridge.

# CHAPTER VIII.

"Hélas! hélas! que la mort est amère!
Hier encore nous étions si joyeux—
Adieu, Marie!  Adieu, ma pauvre mère!
Dejà je sens appesantir mes yeux."
*Le Soldat Mourant.*

"Marching, marching, ever marching
'Neath the Sun-God's madd'ning glow—
Soul-sick, weary, staggering, parching,
Following still a phantom foe."
ANON.

AFTER crossing the Mukundra Pass, we came to Beheeborra, where the faithless *vox populi* said we were to halt for a day, as General Roberts and the rest of the division were waiting there.  Besides our own brigade, which consisted of 1st Bombay Lancers, 8th Hussars, 3rd Troop Horse Artillery, her Majesty's 95th, and the 10th Native Infantry, we brought in the heavy guns, which had been obliged to halt for a day at Mukundra, in order that the bullocks might recover the shaking and exertion of drawing the siege-train up the Pass. Before finally arranging our tent, I thought it would be advisable to ascertain whether the report respecting the halt was true or not.  The Colonel's answer took me aback. "Halt! Oh, no. On the contrary, the Brigadier has just informed me that we start to-morrow morning in pursuit of the escaped rebels; that is to say, we are to march down to the Grand Trunk Road, as Sir Hugh Rose is advancing, and requires our brigade to protect his rear. We are ordered to send our sick to Neemuch, and to take provisions for a month." So we found that there was more work to be done before going into cantonments, but we little thought at that time how long it would last. We were comforted by the assurances of all the officers who had previously served in India, that it was impossible that we could remain out another month, as the heat would render campaigning impossible. " I remember," said one officer, " being out in the Punjaub until the 28th April, but that was quite unprecedented."

At two o'clock on the following morning (April 25th), the brigade marched for Jubra-Patten. We were told the distance was eight miles; we found it considerably nearer eighteen. Just before reaching camp, we crossed a branch of the Chumbul River by two fords, and most delicious and refreshing was the cool water, in which our horses pawed and splashed, and buried their dusty heads. Turkey possesses a great advantage over this country in its clear fountains, with their large troughs of pure water, which are immeasurably superior to the tanks and wells of India. The water of the latter, nearly

H

always more or less stagnant, is often the colour
of mud; and I have sometimes fancied that it has
anything but a cleansing effect upon the skin. Our
bheestie frequently goes to four or five wells, before
he can procure water fit to drink; and it usually
has an earthy taste, which, if not unwholesome, is at
any rate excessively disagreeable. When poured into
the common earthenware "chatty" of the country,
which is very porous, and placed in the hot wind,
it becomes almost as cold as through the agency of
ice. The thermometer has now risen to 114° to
115°. I hastily took up a bunch of keys which
had been lying for some time on the table in the
tent, exposed to the hot wind, and had to drop them
very quickly, for they burnt my fingers.

This is the anniversary of the day on which we
had left England for Constantinople and Bulgaria
in 1854, and of that on which we had embarked at
Ismid to return home in 1856.

Jubra-Patten is a large fortified town, well supplied
with water, and possessing really fine gardens, in
which, notwithstanding the heat, we were tempted
to stroll at evening-tide. We are unable to halt here
on account of the Rajah's troops. They must be a
lawless set, for their own suzerain is afraid of them,
and earnestly requested that none of our soldiers
might be allowed to communicate with them, or to
visit their camp. He will not admit them into his
town at any time, and at night he shuts his gates,

and points his guns on their lines. It was half
hoped that an excuse might be found for attacking
them; but nothing of the kind occurred, so we
continued our wanderings, crossing a dry, but very
wide river bed, believed to be a tributary of the
Chumbul. At Usawarra, where we halted, after
eight days' consecutive marching, we thought ourselves fortunate in securing a group of trees, beneath
which the Brigadier and staff and several officers
pitched their tents. The shade was an inestimable
blessing in the daytime, but we soon learned the
disadvantages of sleeping where a free current of
air cannot be obtained. I spent the whole night
in alternately bathing, walking about, and fanning
myself with an English fan, for we had not at that
time even a hand-punkah. We are now in the
Bengal Presidency, and many of our servants, who
look upon the frontier of Bombay as upon the
boundary of another world, give indications of a
desire to run, which obliges us to watch them closely.
An officer having incautiously mentioned, in the
hearing of one of them, who understood English, that
we should not return to Neemuch, first caused the
alarm.

Our next halt, after three days, marked by no
particular incident, was at Chuppra, a large town on
the borders of Tonk and Gwalior. We forded two
rivers during the last march from Berodi. After
passing the second, which was deeper than usual,

and in the middle of which a cart, drawn by two bullocks, was upset, we met the chief man resident in Chuppra.   He is secretary to the Nawab of Tonk, and had come out with an escort of fifty men to conduct us to our encamping ground.   The foot soldiers of his party were armed with swords and matchlocks, and the cavalry carried blunderbusses. They rode the horses of the country, and the costumes of some of them were wondrously grotesque. The Secretary himself was handsomely dressed in a green velvet head-dress, very like the cowl of a chimney-pot, and a black robe extensively embroidered.   One of his officers rode a trained charger, taught to adopt a showy and graceful prance, which had, however, entirely superseded his natural action. I inquired if he were for sale, and was told that " no price could be put upon him, but, if he pleased me, he was mine as a gift."   The inhabitants, who manifested a very friendly spirit, informed us that Lalla, with a body-guard of rebels, had lately passed within six miles of them, and that he was supposed to be still in the neighbourhood; but as he is not permitted to enter the villages, either here or in Gwalior, it is presumed that his followers must be starving in the jungle.

On the evening of our arrival at Chuppra the Secretary courteously sent an elephant, that I might ride on it to see the town.   The sonorous voice of a large bell attached to his trappings, announced his

approach. He was an enormous fellow, although
still youthful (being only fifty years old), with an
expression almost ludicrous, of cunning and wisdom,
in his little bright, twinkling eyes. His approach
to our tent frightened the horses nearly out of their
senses. To our disappointment there was no ladder
or means of climbing into the howdah, unless by
scrambling up his trunk or his tail, so he had to
return the way he came, trumpeting to show his
satisfaction, and bundling himself off with more
expedition than grace. There is something very
laughable in the hurried gait of an elephant. His
hocks bending inward, like the human knee, suggest
the idea of an old man shuffling along in a hurry.

There are here very handsome stone tanks and
wells, containing deliciously clear water. On the
last day of our halt, by special and urgent invitation, we accompanied the Brigadier and a large
party of the natives to the gardens of the Ressildar,
" to see the fountains play." We rode through the
ill-constructed and unsavoury town, and, after many
ups and downs, came to the gardens, which were
thronged with an expectant crowd. On our arrival,
five or six jets began dribbling into a small basin
in the most melancholy way, to the admiration and
delight of the inhabitants, whose imaginations were
not haunted by the memories of Sydenham or Ver-
sailles. The next day we

"Folded our tents like the Arabs;"

and as the heat of the sun renders a standing camp
intolerable after a few days, we were not sorry to
change the ground, and march towards Shikarpoor.
The first ten miles were smooth enough; but we
then descended abruptly, and came to three streams,
forming in the rainy season the one enormous body
of the Parbuttee river, the bed of which is composed
of rock and large loose stones, affording very uncertain footing. We passed these " uncanny " fords
with only one horse down, and camped in some very
pretty and green jungle on the other side.

The next morning Brigadier Smith started with
the Bombay Lancers, four guns of the Horse
Artillery, one troop (or rather two half troops) of
the 8th Hussars, the greater part of the 95th and
10th N. I. to Pardoun, in the hope of coming
across the rebel force and capturing Lalla, who
was reported to be hidden in a cave in that neighbourhood. The expedition resulted in the capture
of an elephant, and, I believe, two guns. The rebels,
aware that they were pursued, fled just in time to
save themselves, leaving their spoil in the hands of
the pursuers.

Whilst the Brigadier and the greater part of the
force were gone to Pardoun, the remainder re-
crossed the rocky fords, and moved out of the thick
jungle, which was reported to contain tigers, encamping on open ground close to the village of Shikarpoor,
which owes its name to the quantity of large game

in its vicinity, Shikar in Hindostanee meaning, I believe, sport, and Shikaree sportsmen.

On the third day of our halt, while my husband and I were angling for little fishes in the Parbuttee, Lieutenant Webster came in from the Brigadier, bearing an order for the force to march at 3 A.M. on Futtyghur. I was too tired with my excursion in the sun to be able to start before daybreak, and then my mind was full of uneasiness about certain bottles of lemonade and ginger beer, which I feared would be broken if trusted upon the back of a camel. Those who have campaigned in an Indian summer will enter into my anxieties, and can judge how tenderly the bottles were laid in a circular basket filled with hay, and how carefully they were deposited in a corner of the gharry. Beer we had none: nor sherry, nor vegetables of any description save our old Bulgarian friend, the onion—blest vegetable, that diffuses its odour over most of the desert places of the earth. We expected to suffer a good deal from the want of necessary supplies, nor were we deceived. After traversing a rocky, precipitous and slippery road, we encamped beneath some trees close to the Fort of Futtyghur, from which the Rajah fired a *feu-de-joie* at our approach.

The Brigadier, whom we found here, informed us that our destination was again changed, and that Sepree, a small station in the Gwalior territory, sixty miles from Jhansi, and situated north-east of

Mhow, was to be our quarters during the rains. All
hope of shelter from the hot weather we have abandoned.   The heat is now at its highest, the thermometer ranging up to 118° to 119°.   Bungalows,
at least the ruins of them, are reported to exist at
Sepree; and as it is upon the Trunk Road, we begin
to hope that it may be possible even during the rains
to get up supplies from Bombay.   We despair of
obtaining all our own special comforts left at Deesa;
linen, dresses, gloves, writing paper, books, boots,
lamps, &c.;  indeed we shall be lucky if we see
them next year.

We left Futtyghur by a stony nullah, through
which it was scarcely possible to drag the guns;
and, after about five miles, reached Jaighur, where
we awaited our baggage in the friendly shelter of a
temple overlooking a shaded stream, in which the
men were soon busily engaged fishing; and with a
very rude kind of rod, one of them landed a large
water tortoise and  some spotted fish resembling
trout.

The next morning, at 3 A.M., we resumed our march
and halted at Goonah, a station on the Grand Trunk
Road, with several bungalows, the ruinous condition
of which gave evidence of the ravages of the mutineers.   As we approached, we were met by Captain
Mayne and an escort of the Irregular Horse he
commands.   We were struck with the soldier-like
appearance of the party, and with the superior class

of horses they rode.  One of the native officers, a
large stout man with a decoration on his breast,
comes from Delhi, where he possesses considerable
property.  Every effort had been made to induce
him to abandon his allegiance to the English, but in
vain.  He was tempted and threatened by turns,
and at last his property was destroyed.  His loyalty
and courage have gained for him the confidence of
his commanding officers, and the sympathy and
admiration of all to whom his history is known.
Captain Mayne—whose family and mine are acquainted, as I afterwards discovered—showed us
every attention and kindness, and endeavoured as
far as possible to make us forget our harassing
march.  While sitting in the cool shade of his
spacious Bengal tents, he recounted to us the story
of his own and his wife's escape from the mutineers—
a story full of anxiety and dread on his part, and of
deep suffering and almost loss of life on hers; for,
forty-eight hours after she was aroused in the middle
of the night, and compelled to conceal herself in the
garden until her husband could convey her to a
carriage, her child was born.  How little we know
of the cases of individual suffering these mutinies
have caused!

Not content with burning the bungalows, the
rebels defaced the tomb of a child, the daughter of
Mr. Belton, formerly in the Contingent here.  In
times of peace a bullock train runs from Bombay to

Agra along the Trunk Road, and even now we found the advantage of being upon it; as at Mhow, only two days post from Goonah, there are several Parsee shops where all kinds of stores can be procured. We expected to remain here for three days, and then to proceed up the Trunk Road to Sepree, only about sixty-five miles further in a northerly direction. But the 15th of May brought the frustration of these hopes.

About five o'clock in the afternoon of that day a party of natives rode into camp, bringing the information that the rebels, to the number of 6,000, had assembled and retaken Chandaree, a fortified town from whence Sir Hugh Rose had ejected them in the previous month of March. The fort was then garrisoned by the soldiers of Scindia, Maharajah of Gwalior, and the guns left in position. When the rebels attacked it, these men, after losing about a hundred of their number, ran away, leaving the enemy in possession of fort and guns. Brigadier Smith, upon receipt of this intelligence, lost no time in putting himself in communication both with Sir Hugh Rose and with General Roberts, as its occupation by a rebel force not only affected the town of Chandaree, but rendered the road between Goonah and Jhansi unsafe.

We have just had an instance of the wonderful things women can do. Mrs. Cotgrave, the wife of an officer in the 3rd Europeans, who was stationed at

Jhansi, and had obtained permanent employment there, determined to join her husband. With a little graceful and delicate child of four years old, and her ayah, she left Poona, and travelled by bullock train to Mhow. Here great difficulties were made, and reasonably, on the part of the authorities, as there was danger in allowing her to proceed. Fearing she would be detained, she left Mhow one night unexpectedly, and travelled in a gharry without an escort of any kind. As they were passing through thick jungle, the gharry, with its helpless freight of two women and a little girl, broke down. The native cart, containing the baggage, had gone on, and was some distance in front. Mrs. Cotgrave's fear of tigers and wild beasts was very great; but she told me that she sat by the wayside during more than an hour, with her little child held tightly in her arms, and trembling with fear, for the jackals were screaming round her with their frightful and unearthly laugh, while the gharry wallah mended the cart. After many delays and adventures, she reached Goonah; and I had the satisfaction of hearing, some time afterwards, that she had rejoined her husband at Jhansi in safety. On the 18th May, we shifted our camp, which the sun was rendering unsavoury; and on the 20th May, we again started on our pilgrimage; this time bound to Chandaree, to dislodge the rebel occupants of the fort. The Brigade was divided; a part of the force consisting of Bom-

bay Lancers, and some of the 10th N. I. going to
Kollariss, near Sepree, to keep the Trunk Road
open, while the rest marched first on Pinnigutti.
Here we were encamped on an open plain to the
east of the Sind River, which we forded just before
we set up our tents.

Many of the rebels who fled from Kotah are now
forming part of the garrison at Chandaree, and the
newspapers are demanding an explanation of their
escape.  No place in this part of the country appears
to be secure.  Colonel Whitelock, coming down from
Agra, was shot on the Trunk Road about four days
since, having fallen in with a body of rebels.  We
have been gratified by reading in one of the Indian
papers a just tribute to Brigadier Smith's column,
and to the courage with which it has supported the
trials of a most harassing march.  The 95th are,
many of them, now obliged to wear native shoes,
their own being entirely worn out.  Some of the
10th N. I. have been despatched from Goonah to
Jubra-Patten, to bring up supplies of shoes and
boots.  But when will they rejoin us, or where?
In the meantime the 95th must march on, footsore and weary, as best they can.  The doctors fear
that scurvy will show itself on account of the absence of nourishing food, beer, and, more particularly, of sleep.

We might almost have been said to have groped
our way to Chandaree, so uncertain, unsatisfactory,

and contradictory was the information afforded to
the Brigadier. On one point, however, all seem
agreed, namely, that the rebels are in force.

On the 21st, we marched to Shahdowra, reaching
our camp at about half-past five A.M., and so being
housed before the sun acquired much power.

On the 24th May, the Queen's birthday, we advanced to Jharee, and, whilst on the march, came to
villages which had been plundered but a few hours
previously by five hundred of the rebels, who were
reported to be encamped on the other side of the
river, on the banks of which we were to set up our
tents.

Our fighting instincts were once more aroused.
We fully hoped to come up with, and account for, an
enemy who appeared so close at hand. It is, however, scarcely necessary to say that no opposing
force appeared to interrupt the even tenor of our
way. An extra ration of grog was served out to
the men in honour of the day. The natives, who
rode into camp towards evening, still persisted in the
proximity of our invisible foe. They told the Brigadier of a ghaut, with a fortified gateway, in our next
march, which would probably be defended. One of
the men of the 8th Hussars remarked to-day : " I
should like to see a live rebel; we've been going
after them so long, I begin to doubt if there are any
at all." Although thick jungle, ghaut, and gateway
would all be in favour of our enemies, very few were

sanguine as to meeting them, though all concurred in hoping that fortune would befriend us. Our Brigadier is so beloved for his unselfishness, kindness of heart, and urbanity of manner, that every one desires a victory on his account, as well as on their own. The strong winds preceding the monsoon had now been blowing for two or three days, and we were in hourly dread of the commencement of the rain. In that case, good-bye to all comfort, or even locomotion. Had the heavens unlocked their flood-gates at this time, we must just have remained where we were; for the poor attenuated camels that pervaded our camps, wandering with silent footsteps, like ghosts, could never have transported our baggage for another march. Twenty-four hours' rain would, moreover, have made it impossible to cross the Betwa River.

On the 25th May we left Khorwassan at daylight, and marched in search of the ghaut and gateway. The gateway proved a fiction, but we crossed a wide river with banks so steep and difficult that it would have been an admirable place for acting on the defensive. The jungle all through the march was so thick as to necessitate strong flanking parties on each side of the track; and six prisoners, whom we captured the day before, persisted in asserting that it was haunted by the mutinous forces. A singular cluster of tombs, with plain Grecian porticos supported on rows of pillars, and tall bulbous roofs,

crowned the river bank. The Brigadier and Bri-
gade-Major each took possession of a house in the
village. We preferred our own tent to the by no
means tempting-looking rooms, notwithstanding that
the Brigadier courteously offered us his house. We
halted nine miles from Chandaree, without having
seen an enemy; but soon afterwards an exciting
scene of a different kind occurred. The greatest
animosity exists between Arab horses and the little
ponies of the country, commonly called Tattoos.
Some of these wretched animals belonging to the
grass-cutters and camp followers, strayed into the
lines of the Horse Artillery. In a few minutes their
whole camp was in an uproar. The troop horses
struggled, and screamed, and fought as though they
were possessed. Every man, whether native or
European, ran to join in the furious fray; for to
quell it was impossible. Horse after horse broke
loose, and galloped wildly away with yards of rope
and picket-posts dangling at their heels. Those that
could not fasten on the ponies, rushed at each other,
and fought on their own score. The combatants
were knocked down, trampled upon, and torn amid
an accompaniment of the most fiendish yells. Order
was restored when the belligerents were tired, and
a long list of casualties was sent in to the Brigadier;
all the mischief being set down to the unfortunate
and suffering ponies, which had strayed in search of
food. Three horses were very severely injured, and

limped along for many a day behind the column, in
the care of their ghorawallahs.

We met with a misfortune at Goonah, in the
lameness of my strong and good-tempered horse
Prince. He ran a splinter into the coronet of his
off fore foot, whilst going at a foot-pace along the
Trunk Road, and being unable to put the wounded
foot to the ground, he was left in the kind charge of
Captain Mayne. For a long time I used to miss his
large black eyes whenever I went to visit his com-
panions; and my regret was hardly dissipated, even
when Bobby, the most independent and consequen-
tial of all little round-faced terriers, condescended to
leave his master, Sir John Hill, our then Brigade-
Major, and to honour me with a visit which he was
careful not to make too long.

We expected on the following day to appear before
Chandaree, but " the even tenor of our way " was
interrupted by a violent storm. The breeze, which
had been blowing strongly all the morning, became
by noon a sort of burning hurricane ; and at four
o'clock, after the thunder had given a preparatory
growl, down came the rain. I scarcely remember
to have seen a fiercer squall, for the time it lasted.
Tents went down like ninepins; our hospital was the
first to go, and the poor sick men were transferred to
the table of the mess tent. The Horse Artillery and
95th mess tents followed, smashing in their fall glass
and china, precious, because not to be replaced.

Several private tents were prostrated, and we feared greatly that the one we occupied would go also; and it would have done so, if all the establishment had not held on to the ropes and flies.

Of course there was an end of marching at 3 A. M., as the camels, fearfully diminished in numbers and in strength, could hardly stagger along even with light loads and in a light soil. We were, therefore, compelled to wait until the tents were dry. At about half-past nine we began to strike, and at eleven commenced to march. It was imperative to move on, as we were in thick jungle, surrounded by the enemy, and within nine miles of their stronghold; but the march, directly and indirectly, cost several lives. Two men of the 95th were struck down by the sun, and perished where they fell. One poor fellow dropped backwards as if shot, just as I rode up, and in a few moments the convulsive action commenced in all his limbs; his lips and face became black almost before life was extinct. The men of the 95th on this day, and for some time after, marched in their scarlet jackets. The fatigue of walking in such heat is enormous, and when to that is added a close-fitting cloth dress, of course it must be doubled. It seems to me most wanton to sacrifice life to appearance in such a way.

The calculation is that each European soldier costs more than one hundred pounds to equip and send out to this country. Surely, then, from economical,

I

if not for any higher motives, everything should be done to alleviate his sufferings, and to give him a chance for his life. I would myself on no account venture out in the sun with a forage cap and thin white cover on my head, such as the men wear; but when to that is added the dress made for and suited to an English climate, the want of common sense becomes still more apparent.*

The 8th Hussars march in stable jackets, cloth overalls, and forage caps with covers—even a hotter dress than that worn by the infantry; and the officers, and most of the men, have sheepskins on their saddles, the heat and discomfort of which are very great; but being mounted, they have not to make the same exertions as a foot soldier.

The dress of the 3rd troop of Horse Artillery contrasts pleasantly enough with those which I have described. Officers and men wear the helmet covered with white, thickly padded round the temples, loose white serge jackets over their shirts, and regimental overalls. They have no sheepskins, which make the saddles of the Hussars a penance to sit on.

About half-past three we halted before Chandaree, and took up our ground. Our march was of necessity slow, as the road lay through more than one mountain pass, and infantry in skirmishing order

* The 95th have since been supplied with light and suitable clothing.

were sent out to clear the heights. Lieutenant
Pierce, with a party of the 10th N. I., took some
few prisoners who were lurking about. A reconnoitring party went out with the Brigadier as soon
as the ground was taken up, and it was quickly discovered that if no rebels were to be seen outside the
walls, there were plenty of them within. They
fired with tolerable precision upon the Brigadier's
party, and the Quartermaster-general very narrowly
escaped being wounded in the foot, the strap being
torn from his overall by a bullet. Working parties
went out at dusk, to make the road passable for the
guns to get into position. The fortifications looked
ugly enough, as the breach made by Sir Hugh Rose
was strongly repaired, and we had only 6-pounder
field guns and a couple of twelve pound howitzers,
wherewith to make another. I was thoroughly tired
out with my long ride in the sun, and slept as though
there were no rebels in the world. Colònel Blake
had kindly offered to show me a place from which I
could watch all the operations of the siege, and I
went to sleep, fully intending to avail myself of his
offer, but the next morning I did not wake until six,
when I heard two guns fired slowly one after the
other. I soon learnt that these were the guns of
the Horse Artillery, and that they had fired upon an
empty town. At midnight the mutinous force had
fled from the place, leaving us to take possession
without the opportunity of a shot or a blow. So

long as the secret intelligence department is inadequately paid, the rebels must draw great advantage and impunity from our ignorance. No native thinks it worth his while to afford information which may endanger his life for the sake of three or four rupees, whereas he might be tempted to run a risk for 200 or 300. Meantime our servants are acting as spies for our enemies. A ghorawallah, belonging to one of the troops of the 8th Hussars, deserted soon after we left Deesa. He was found at Kotah; but as he gave a good account of himself, and the regiment was in want of ghorawallahs, he was taken back. Shortly after we left Kotah he deserted again and was found in Chandaree, where, with six others, he was shortly afterwards hanged. Two days after the flight of the rebels, a letter was received, stating that the Ranee of Teary, anxious to manifest her friendly feeling towards the English, had despatched a force of 3,000 men, under command of Captain Maclean, to join us. As this force was supposed to be marching from the direction towards which the rebels had fled, we hoped that it might fall in with them; but day by day went by, and we heard no more tidings of it.

Sir Hugh Rose appears to possess, in an eminent degree, what the French term " *un talent pour la gloire*," and his progress through Central India must have been most triumphant. But so scanty is the information which reaches us, that

we know little beyond our own adventures, and
that little, as in the Crimea, chiefly through the
English papers. On the afternoon of the day
following the flight of the rebels (May 27th), we
rode with Sir John Hill through the town and fort,
which are surrounded by natural fortifications consisting of precipitous hills, between which lie deep
vallies clothed with green. In these are massive and
beautiful tombs, standing singly and in clusters, close
to the walls of the city. We have seen no town in
India which can compare with Chandaree, and no
ruins which equal in beauty its temples houses, and
decaying tombs. Tall gateways carved with delicate
tracery, and a large temple adorned with elaborate
carvings and filled with gods in various coloured
marbles, give an idea of the former splendours of the
place. But now the city is silent and deserted;
our horses' footfalls ring unanswered through the
streets, and the presence of one or two decrepit men
and women creeping in and out of the houses only
makes the desolation more apparent. We mounted
its steep streets and gained the rugged road that
wound upwards to the fort. Passing through the
latter we rode to the breach, and saw where the guns
of the Horse Artillery had been placed in the morning, and also the position of the heavy guns, during
Sir Hugh Rose's bombardment. We returned in
the light of sunset, and I felt saddened and depressed,
for the spell of the silent city was upon me ; its pro-

found and beautiful desolation reminded me of the exclamation of Jeremiah when lamenting over Jerusalem : " How doth the city sit solitary that was full of people !  How is she become as a widow ! "

The place is surrounded by two lines of fortification, the outer one running from hill to hill about a mile and a half in front of the actual city wall.  It was taken by the English somewhere about the year 1815, and the ruins of this outer wall even now bear picturesque testimony to having been effectually breached.  A short distance beyond the outer wall is a ruin, over which we have conjectured in vain.  It is cruciform, and built with double aisles formed of two tiers of arches every way.  Running along the top of the highest tier is a hollow passage, resembling the " nun's walk," or cleristery of our cathedrals. The whole building is ecclesiastical in form and appearance.  But how has the ecclesiastical architecture of Europe found its way into Central India? It stands alone—there are neither figures of gods nor tombs near it.  The roof has given way, and a large tree grows on the top of the wall, from whence the wide span of the centre arch originally sprung. The walls, however, are massive and almost uninjured.

General orders containing a complimentary order respecting " the very brilliant feat of arms of Kotah," have been forwarded to the column.  *There is, however, no mention whatever made of the cavalry, nor of*

*the valuable assistance they afforded to the escaping*
*rebels!*

On the 1st June, Brigadier Smith having heard
nothing further from Captain Maclean and the Teary
Contingent, resolved to break up his camp before
Chandaree and march on Sepree. Cloudy days,
and several smart showers, gave warning that the
end of the fine weather was approaching, and two
large rivers still lay between us and the "haven
where we would be." General Roberts and the rest
of our division have been stationary long ago : and
we were willing to hope that only eight more
marches lay between us and the shelter we had so
long desired. Our native servants also took heart,
and arrived at Mahoulie, where we halted the first
day, more lively than they had been for some time.
We pitched by the side of a river, deep and cool,
lying in the shadow of overhanging trees. A hive
of bees had swarmed in one of them ; and some of
the doolie wallahs (grasscutters), or other necessary
evils of the Indian camp, disturbed them. A scene
of the utmost confusion ensued, the enraged insects
attacking men and horses with the greatest vigour.
Several persons, including three or four officers of
the 8th Hussars, were severely stung about the face,
neck, and hands. We were fortunately not in the
direction taken by the bees, and could laugh in
safety at the energy and speed with which the
victims sought to escape. The old hands, who had

been some time in India, and had profited by past
experience, ran their faces and shoulders into the
thickest bushes they could find, and so escaped
unstung.  The day after, we moved on to Esaghur,
a long and tiresome road, which for the first few
miles lay through a very narrow track in the hills,
where the camels could only pass in single file.
The baggage was, in consequence, so much delayed,
that it was after one o'clock before our tents made
their appearance, and I was indebted for breakfast
to the kindness of Sir John Hill.

Our march was on the ascent the whole way, and
at Esaghur we found ourselves on a firm hard soil,
with a fine breeze, and at a healthy elevation.  On
the following morning, soon after we had reached
our camping ground at Koosnawier, a party
sent in from Colonel Owen, commanding the 1st
Lancers, brought intelligence from which it appeared that the mutiny, far from being nearly
quelled, has assumed a worse aspect.  The Gwalior
Contingent, which revolted last year, having been
joined by reinforcements under Tantia Topee, has
retaken Gwalior, a place of such strength and importance as to be called the "Delhi of Central
India."    Many of Scindia's troops have turned
against him, and he and his family have fled: and
this, when we are within a few days of the rainy
season!  Colonel Owen also stated that a lac and a
half of rupees had arrived at Kollariss for the use

of the brigade; but that the rebels were hovering so thickly round that place and its small protecting force, that he lived in dread of an attempt being made to seize it by overpowering numbers; and requested the Brigadier would rejoin him with all speed. The prospect of the rupees was hailed with joyful exclamations by everybody; as neither officers, men, nor camp followers, had for a month past been paid more than was absolutely necessary to carry them on. Out of shoes, out of money, out of provisions, and getting more and more out of health, it is high time that the column should go into cantonments.

# CHAPTER IX.

"Says Giles: ''Tis mortal hard to go,
   But if so be's I must,
I means to follow arter he
   As goes hisself the first."
                              TOM BROWN.

ON the 5th June we reached Kollariss, and rejoined
the force of lancers and native infantry which had
been detached to keep open the communications
along the Trunk Road. The ill news gathered
strength as we approached Sepree, from which we
are now distant only fourteen miles. The head
man of this place is in great alarm. He urges the
Brigadier to hasten to Sepree, which he tells us we
shall probably find sacked and burned; and, at the
same time, declares most decidedly that he will not
be left behind. He says, "I am not a soldier; I
am a pundit, a scholar. Why should I risk my life
in the hands of these people, whom I absolutely
refuse to serve? I have been brought up with the
English all my life, and have always been on their
side, I cannot now change." In point of fact, the
position of our column resembles very much that
of a ship at sea—we pass through the rebels, and

they close up behind us after we have passed.  A detachment of the 8th Hussars and H. M.'s 95th is to be left at Kollariss to comfort the soul of the Chief, and also to keep the road open and prevent the dâk being stopped.

We started at midnight for Sepree, half expecting to find the place in flames when we arrived.  Everything, however, was tranquil; a large fire lit the horizon on our right hand, but we saw no signs of the enemy.  The Trunk Road was almost as smooth and level as an English turnpike, so much so, that once I was surprised into a canter.  Large trees pointed out the site of the town; and when we reached the cantonment we were all delighted with the beauty of its situation, the handsome, although ruinous bungalows, and the abundant shade.  Our camp was pitched on a shelving ground of hard gravel, abounding with white ants.  On the first morning after we arrived we found one of our carpet-bags nearly eaten through; but the delicious feeling that here we were to sit down and rest, overbalanced all discontent at minor evils.  With what feelings of thankfulness to that good Providence who had " brought us all the way hitherto " did we lie down to sleep that night!  Although, on inspection, the bungalows proved to be in such ruinous condition that it was impossible to occupy them at once, still the situation appeared more and more advantageous, with its good wells, and plenty of them;

its fine light soil, which would not be impassable
with the heaviest rain, and its gardens with flowering shrubs; so we spent three days in peace, and
rest, and self-illusion; but on the fourth day a
messenger arrived with three little screws of paper
hidden away in different parts of his clothing; and
on each of these twisted scraps was an order to
proceed immediately to Gwalior. A despatch from
Sir Hugh Rose soon followed. He, with his division,
was marching on Gwalior from Calpee, and we were
ordered to join Colonels Orr and Hicks, who were
also marching thither, before attempting the Antree
Pass, which lay between us and Gwalior. After
all, we feel that we have become as accustomed
to marching as the eels to their traditionary fate,
and are glad of an opportunity of joining forces
under Sir Hugh Rose. The report, which had
reached us, of his having gone to Poonah, of course
turns out to be false; but the local papers assert
that he has suffered very severely from the effects
of the sun, having been knocked off his horse by
it three times in one day.

On the 10th June, we marched to Suttawarra.
My husband had sprained his ancle on the road from
Kollariss to Sepree, and was plentifully leeched the
evening before; so he had to follow helplessly in
the gharry, which, by the time he reached Suttawarra, had nearly dislocated his bones. My "Pearl"
has had his hoofs much broken, and I was thinking

of taking his shoes off for a month; and "Prince"
is still an invalid, in the care of Captain Mayne, at
Goonah. We had fortunately been able to procure
from a native shopkeeper a small store of beer and
sherry; and on the evening of the 8th, seven cart-
loads of stores came up for the mess from Mhow
before we left. On the day of our arrival, when
our men crowded down to the bazaar, a sepoy of the
7th Gwalior Contingent levelled his musket (an
English one) at a man of the 3rd Troop Horse
Artillery, and fired. Fortunately the cap snapped;
but I never shall forget the excitement with which
the men crowded round their prisoner, and brought
him to the Brigadier's tent. He was there recognised by a trumpeter of the Lancers. He was a tall,
strong man, with a very bad expression of countenance; and I am told he met his death with
profound indifference, mounting the cart of his own
accord, and springing off it, when the noose was
round his neck.

Since the 10th of June, my pen has never been in
my hand. For several days and nights the noise
and stir of the camp have been but as a confused and
troubled dream to me. I have been lying on my
bed unconscious, or communing only with my own
heart. It is sad to lie in pain and weakness amidst
such stirring scenes; and to be so dependent, helpless, and exhausted, as to feel that the sleep of death
would scarcely be sufficiently deep to afford relief.

How vain is all human strength and courage, when in a moment, and in the very midst of our self-reliant pride, the will of God can cast us down and leave us to be helplessly carried hither and thither at the will of others.  A few hours of illness suffice to take away that power of pleasing which gives life such a charm to its possessor.  The face becomes pale and wan—no witticism sparkles from the parched lips—no laughter kindles in the eyes that are filled with ever ready tears.  True heroism is not to ride gallantly amid the braying of trumpets and all the pomp and circumstance of war, but to wrestle alone, in solitary fight, with darkness and the shadow of death.  Many a one may be brave before his fellows, and ride at a gallop to the very cannon's mouth, who would shrink from the sharp arrows of pain, from the weary, lonely watching, and from all the humiliation of soul and body that weakness and illness entail.

From myself, my thoughts wandered to the great ones of old, " who made themselves mountains whereon to stand, and saw the storms of life not above their heads, but rolling far beneath their feet," —and I remembered that they, too, were of the dust.

> " What was their prosperous estate,
> When high, exalted, and elate,
>     With power and pride ?
> What but a transient gleam of light,
> A flame, which glaring in its height,
>     Grew dim and died.

" The noble steed, the harness bright,
  The gallant lord, and stalwart knight
    In rich array,
  Where shall we seek them now ? Alas !
  Like the bright dewdrops on the grass,
    They fade away."

Individual suffering counts for nothing where the movements of an army are concerned. The strong fight through—the weak lie down and die; and the brigade marches on just the same. But, happily, above all, watches the Almighty Power, without whom nothing is strong, and without whose knowledge not a sparrow falls to the ground.

Through the kindness of the Brigadier, and of Lieutenant-Colonel Blake, my dooley was allowed to be carried near the head of the column. It was many days before I was able to sit in my saddle; and, on the first attempt, I fainted from sheer pain.

At Antree, we found Lieutenant-Colonel Hicks, with details of the 71st, 86th, some Hydrabad Contingent (cavalry), a couple of mortars, and some eighteen-pounder guns. We were then nine miles from the place appointed for the Brigade to encamp before Gwalior, in order to co-operate with Sir Hugh Rose. Of course, we expected that the Antree Pass would be defended; but we marched through it without let or hindrance. I was half stifled with dust in my dooley, until we came to an open plain with slight eminences on the left, backed by a high range of hills. On the foremost of the lower emi-

nences, we saw a body of cavalry ; while the enemy
in numbers appeared and disappeared on the ridges
of the more distant heights. Our force was halted,
and drawn up. Brigadier Smith, with a troop of
H. M.'s 8th Hussars, and Lieutenant Harris, of the
Horse Artillery, went off to reconnoitre. We saw
them the whole time going down at an easy gallop.
Pain was forgotten at such an exciting moment, and
I got out of my dooley and stood to watch. When
they approached the hill on which the cavalry was
drawn up, a battery, hitherto masked, opened upon
them, and, as they turned to gallop out of range, we
saw one or two men and horses fall, and a dark spot
remain stationary. Just before the guns opened,
Lieutenant Harris was riding, unconsciously, of
course, straight at the battery, and it was extra-
ordinary that he was not hit. The Brigadier's horse,
slightly wounded in the stifle, fell and rolled over
him, bruising his rider severely on the temple, and
spraining his wrist. He was not one to make the
most of a grievance, and it was not until his face and
hand were swelled and discoloured, that we found
out he had been hurt. As soon as the reconnoitring
party returned, Colonel Blake's troop of Horse Artillery clattered down at a gallop; a squadron of the
8th Hussars followed, as also part of the Lancers,
the 95th and the 18th N. I.

It proved that the enemy's cavalry was drawn up
behind a nullah, wide, deep, and full of water. To

cross this the Horse Artillery had to change their
course, and to find a fordable place; but into it,
without hesitation, rushed Major Chetwode, Lieutenant and Adjutant Harding, weighing over fifteen
stone, and Sir John Hill, whose horse fell and rolled
over him. The rebels, after some smart firing on
both sides, galloped away to the heights, taking their
guns with them. It was said that they fired six-
pound shot out of nine-pound guns, which accounted
for the very long range at which their shot fell.
The 95th and 10th then commenced skirmishing up
the heights, under a heavy fire from an earthwork
battery.

A troop of Lancers and Hussars had been sent out
to scour the plain, and see that none of the rebel
cavalry were lurking about. These, returning at a
gallop in rear of where the baggage camels and
baggage guard were drawn up, caused a momentary
check to the proceedings in front, as it was reported
to the Brigadier that columns of dust were seen in
rear of the baggage, and that the enemy were about
to attack it.

About this time the wounded began dropping in,
and dooleys were seen in the distance, bearing their
freight of pain and blood to where the surgeons were
awaiting them. The first contained poor Berry, a
bandsman of the 8th Hussars, whose leg was so
fearfully shattered that immediate amputation at the
hip was considered necessary; and was, I am told,

K

most skilfully carried out by Dr. Lockwood, 8th
Hussars, the poor patient being under the influence
of chloroform. When first struck, he knew his
wound was mortal, and half an hour after the operation he had ceased to live. Then an artilleryman
came galloping wildly in, with bare head, and
with his shoulder and his horse's quarters splashed
with blood. Happily, however, his wound was
slight; a shot had carried off his helmet and grazed
his head and ear. But more and more came in;
some wounded, some dying of sunstroke; and the
doctors have full employment. Another amputation
this time in the artillery hospital; and still the 95th
and 10th are steadily skirmishing on, and the artillery and cavalry have advanced until they are out
of our sight.

The voices of the guns (how eagerly listened to
by those who were detained by duty or sickness in
the camp!) told us that our force must be gaining
ground, as they became less and less distinct.

Lieutenant Reilly, killed by sunstroke within a
few minutes after having ridden a dashing and eager
charge, was brought into hospital; and later in the
day he, with poor Berry and two other men, one a
non-commissioned officer, was consigned to a hastily-
made grave, with as much care as circumstances
would allow.

About four o'clock came an order for the baggage
to move up three miles, and to halt on the very

heights which in the morning had bristled with the enemy. As soon as my dooley-wallahs had conveyed me to the first height, I met Brigadier Smith, who told me that they had ridden right through the enemy's camp under the Fort; and that if the troops had not been completely exhausted (neither man nor horse had broken fast since the previous evening), and dropping out of their saddles from the extreme heat, he would have routed the whole outlying force, and held the suburbs of the city.

This brilliant day's work was achieved solely by our tried and jaded column. Had Sir Hugh Rose been able to afford them the slightest assistance—had he even sent out one European regiment—they would have destroyed the whole of the enemy's camp. When we took up our position for the night, the evening was drawing in, but not sufficiently to prevent the enemy, who occupied the opposite heights, from annoying us with their shot. I could not help laughing at the effects of the first one that came. It hurt nobody, but pitched in the middle of a cluster of camels and their drivers, causing the most direful confusion and dismay. One fled one way, another ran another. The dooley-wallahs seized their loads, and ran for their lives. But when it became dark, and the shot still came, it was not quite so amusing. Everything was avoided that could attract the notice of the enemy; no tents were pitched, no fires were lighted, and no fires entailed no dinners.

As I had taken nothing but a biscuit and a cup of tea, kindly given to me by Lieutenant Mayne, 1st Lancers, at seven A.M., and another cup of tea charitably sent me at four P.M. by an utter stranger, Dr. Brodrick, I started in the dark in search of something to eat; and meeting my husband and Lieutenant Hanbury, both on the sick report, who were on the same errand, we at last found the messman, and secured two bottles of beer, as hot as though it had been boiled, but still better than nothing. After this I betook myself to the gharry, and my husband to his dooley alongside. We then slept until morning, when, as there was no firing on the camp, and the sun was very hot, the tents were pitched. There was not a blade of grass for horses or bullock, but there was a little grain left, and we hoped that they would, at any rate, get a day's rest.

About eleven o'clock, as soon as the enemy saw that we had made ourselves comfortable, down came a shot close to our tent. Another and another followed; then they fired from another gun at the horses of the artillery, and afterwards at some carts in a nullah close by. For two hours they kept harassing us in this way, until at last an 18-pound gun, with two elephants, was sent on to our advanced height. I was not sorry when I heard his glorious voice, for it was too bad to allow the enemy to knock our camp about as they pleased. The trail of the carriage, however, broke soon after our great friend was brought into action; and when he became silent the rebels resumed their fire, killing several horses, one in the midst of our picket, and wounding the wife of an artillery ghora-wallah. Towards evening we rode out to see what we could, and as we were returning a shell burst so directly over our heads that it was a wonder to myself as well as to others who saw it, that neither my husband nor I was hurt. Not long after, whilst I was superintending the packing of our camels, the load of one of them was struck by a shot nearly spent. The animal spun round and round two or three times, and then fell down, but was unhurt.

About ten o'clock the next morning Sir Hugh Rose's force made its appearance, and an order was given to shift the camp round the spur of the hill, where it would be safe from shot. The thermometer all this time ranged at 114°. In less than half an hour after we had moved our tent the shot came whistling over and about it, and all hands had to be again mustered to unpitch. Finding that quiet and comfort were out of the question, we mounted our horses, my husband with great difficulty, for his foot was enormously swelled and very painful, and rode across the heights to see what the movement in Sir Hugh's camp signified, little thinking that we were to be the spectators of a battle. All the artillery and heavy guns were moving out of camp, also the cavalry, and plenty of infantry. Our brigade was nearly all out, and we presently saw the 86th and 95th ascending the hill in skirmishing order to take revenge upon our enemies for the mischief done by their guns. We joyfully watched them ascending, for we knew that if Europeans cannot stand against our infantry, no native Indians would entertain the notion for a moment. The Horse Artillery and cavalry were now slowly and steadily advancing towards the large, level plain in front of the stern fort of Gwalior, which rises on a rock, abruptly, something after the manner of Stirling Castle. Sir Hugh Rose was very unwilling at first to bring on a general action, but soon saw that unless he drove the enemy forward they would steal round the hills, and fall upon our rear. The infantry gained the heights, routed the rebels, took their guns, turned them on the flying foe, and under their cover, the cavalry got quickly into the plain. Here we followed them, in time to see the 8th Hussars, at least one squadron of them, led by Captain Heneage and Captain Poore, fully atoning for their forced inactivity at Kotah. The rebels were driven quite to the other end of the plain, amongst some trees; the artillery then rattled in, and gave them such sharp practice, in spite of the grape and shrapnel they sent in return, that they were soon glad to leave. Presently, away they went, hundreds of

horsemen, racing as though they were after a fox,
and closely followed by the 14th Light Dragoons
and 8th Hussars. In the battery from which I
was watching there were two 18-pounders, one of
which was quickly swung round, and opened on the
flying mass. Unhappily its range was too short.
Away they sped, and soon dense clouds of dust hid
from our eyes the last traces of that discomfited
host. It then became necessary to scour the plains,
lest any should be found lurking in houses or under
topes of trees. The impulse to accompany the
cavalry and artillery was irresistible; and I never,
never shall forget the throbbing excitement of that
short gallop, when the horse beneath one, raging in
his fierce strength, and mad with excitement, scarcely
touched the ground. We halted beyond the enemy's
cantonment, and underneath the grim walls of the
fort. Of course we expected some remonstrative
guns to open on us, or some notice to be taken of
this very forward movement; but all was silent
and still. We could not account for this inaction
on the part of the gunners in the fort.

It was now growing dusk; and as nothing more
could be done, my husband and I turned our horses'
heads back to the camp, promising to send out a camel
laden with provisions for the officers, and another
for the men, as neither had broken fast since breakfast, and there was no prospect of their doing so
within any definite time. We learned afterwards

that several of the mutineers, who were unable to get
away with the main rush, had hidden themselves
in the village, or rather cantonment, through which
we passed, but they did not fire upon us, dreading,
perhaps, the consequences of attracting notice. It
was just by these cantonments that Sergeant Lynch,
paymaster clerk, 8th Hussars, was shot during the
action of the 17th. Of course, holding the appointment he did, he had no business to have gone into
action; but it must be difficult for any soldier who
is worthy of the name to keep himself back in the
day of battle: at any rate, there they all were,
orderly-room clerk, schoolmaster sergeant, and paymaster clerk; of these volunteers one was killed,
and a second wounded, in endeavouring to save
the life of his comrade. The bodies of several of
our non-commissioned officers and men who had
fallen the day before were found in the cantonments mutilated. One was lying near some
burnt haystacks, half roasted away; Sergeant Lynch
was beheaded; and three others were discovered in
the Lushkar, also with their heads cut off, and
hanging up by their heels. Our infantry on the
evening of that triumphant day penetrated into the
town of Gwalior, and in several cases were met
by the servants of the Maharajah, bringing them
champagne and beer—a most grateful draught for
the parched throats of those stalwart, grim, and
dusty men.

On our return I found myself terribly exhausted and in great suffering, for I could not sit in my saddle, unless under circumstances of strong excitement, without tears being forced from my eyes by sheer pain. When the *reveillée* sounded at four on the following morning, we became aware of the deep and stifling dust, which seemed more than human philosophy could endure. My charpoy, hair, and eyes, as well as the breakfast that we managed to secure before starting, were merely a compound of dust. The water in the bath it was impossible to use—not only was it the colour of bitter beer, but the dust floated in a scum upon the top. So I crept on to the back of my pretty little horse, sobered after his work and scanty food of the previous day, and, with my husband and Lieutenant Hanbury, both invalids like myself, moved after the force, which had been ordered to encamp by the side of the fort, and in front of the town of Gwalior. On asking what had occurred, I was told that about two hours after we had left the division of Horse Artillery, they were ordered back to camp. The rebels had fled; but although the soldiers were gone, the guns of the fort kept on firing at irregular and distant intervals during the night. In the morning when the troops went in to garrison the place, they discovered some eleven or twelve fanatics, only two of whom knew how to fire a cannon. They were very soon despatched by the infantry, having proved that, like the six hundred Marseillaise immortalized by Carlyle, they "knew how to die." The two men had spent the night in going round to the various guns, all of which were loaded, and appending slow matches to them, so that, of course, when the match burned down they exploded. We reached the fort in time to see the greater part of the procession, consisting of Scindia, his family, and retainers, who, escorted by a guard of honour, composed of 8th Hussars and 14th Light Dragoons, returned in state to occupy the palace, from which he had fled some weeks previously, and to resume the government. Sir Hugh Rose, the brigadiers, and their respective staffs in full dress, accompanied the Maharajah on his entry. He dismounted, entered his palace, and ascended to the durbar, leaning on the arm of Sir Hugh. Various ceremonials, more tedious than interesting, were gone through. Betel-nut and rose-water were handed round, the whole assembly was crowned with garlands of flowers, proclamations were made, and Scindia was reseated on his throne in the presence of all the chief men of Gwalior.

Our first care, on shifting ground, was for the poor sick; their numbers had increased terribly during the fatigue and exposure of the last three days. In the Hussar Hospital alone, for one wing of the regiment, there were thirty-six patients, all suffering more or less from prostration of strength. For them there was no remedy, but absolute quiet and perfect rest. The total of the 95th Regiment then in hospital was eighty-five men, and the only two medical officers, at that time attached to them, were also sick. It was afterwards found necessary to augment the medical staff for this regiment to a principal medical officer and three assistant-surgeons. None, but those who have gone through it, can tell the effects of a hot-weather campaign upon the nervous system. The constitution becomes completely shattered and broken up. Our own sick (8th Hussars) were placed in some handsome buildings, surrounded by a large garden, a little to the left of the camp; and Dr. Lockwood, whose skill and kindness of heart made him of great value, took up his residence in a temple, within the same green and pleasant enclosure. The centre building in this extensive garden was left unoccupied, as it had evidently been resorted to by the wounded rebels during the three previous days, the walls and floor being splashed, and, in some places, covered with blood. After all, I do not imagine that the slaughter on the 17th and 19th June was very great. We saw a good many bodies lying about in different directions, some of them bearing marks of frightful sword-cut wounds, but none of the masses that we remember in the foughten fields of the Crimea.

The next morning, four-and-twenty hours after the evacuation of Gwalior by Tantia Topee and his followers, the Agra Brigade, under command of

Brigadier General Napier, started in pursuit; they were reinforced by a squadron of the 8th Hussars, and Sir Hugh Rose followed with a part of his division.  Very heavy firing was heard by us in camp, from about nine A.M. till noon.  We could tell that some severe engagement was going on, and later in the day the information was brought that the rebels had made a stand at an entrenched camp about twelve miles from Gwalior.  A division of the 3rd Troop Horse Artillery, under command of Lieutenant Le Cocq, with a troop of 8th Hussars, went out later in the day to reinforce.

The bodies of several sepoys and horses lying about in the vicinity of our camp soon made it advisable that we should change our ground. Before doing so my husband and I had the pleasure of dining with Sir Hugh Rose, whom we had not had an opportunity of meeting since we came into this country, and it was pleasant to renew an agreeable acquaintance commenced in the Crimea.  He shows that the Indian sun is no respecter of persons, for he looks worn out with this deadly climate.

The Brigadier and Staff, including my husband, took possession of three bungalows which had served as habitations for the native officers of the Contingent.  They were situated in front of the cantonments through which the cavalry and artillery passed on the evening of the 19th, after the rebels had fled. They were built of mud, plastered, and very thickly

thatched or chuppered, and consisted of a small dark
room in the centre and a verandah open on each
side. The strong breeze, herald of the monsoon,
began to blow on the morning after we had established ourselves in these residences, and however
much reason we had to rejoice in the thick roof
over our heads, we soon found that the whirlwinds
of dust which came sweeping and swirling through
the building, without any intermission day or night,
superadded to the intolerable heat a nuisance still
more insufferable. This, together with a matter
that was causing me considerable worry and annoyance, made our residence in the native officer's hut
at Gwalior painful beyond words. However, time
and the hour wear through the longest day, and we
soon changed our camp, although perhaps not much
for the better. Whilst the arrangements for shifting
quarters were in progress our squadron came in,
bringing with it the welcome news that not only
had they overtaken the fugitives as before recorded,
but they had taken from them five-and-twenty guns,
besides inflicting heavy loss. These, with the guns
taken in Gwalior and its neighbourhood, amount to
sixty in all. The loss on our side has been totally
inadequate to the work done. The 8th Hussars lost
one officer (from sunstroke), Lieutenant Reilly, and
seven non-commissioned officers and men. The 3rd
troop of Horse Artillery had one man killed, and I
believe, three wounded, and the loss of H. M.'s

96th was proportionately slight. The Bombay Lancers sustained a loss in a favourite young officer, Lieutenant Mills, shot through the body. The sun fought against us, and proved nearly as formidable as the guns of the enemy.

On the 24th of June we shifted camp about two miles. Gwalior and Agra are considered the two hottest places in Central India, and the ground to which we removed, barren, sandy, and surrounded by hills, afforded no advantages in the way of coolness. The rains, too, it was evident from the appearance of the sky, would not keep off much longer, and Brigadier Smith was anxious to start on his march to Sepree before they rendered his doing so next to impracticable. Delay, however, intervened, and on the 25th of June the thunder began to peal, and down came the rain. We were new to a tropical climate, and I shall not easily forget the first day of the Indian rains; all the morning the heat had been intense, the sky glittering and bright, and the birds gasping with open beaks. Rapidly the sky became overcast; and almost without further warning, in a moment, came down such a pour of rain that I can only compare it to a waterspout. The plain, which a quarter of an hour before had made us miserable with clouds of dust, was now a pool of muddy water, which in half an hour reached the knees of those who were adventurous enough to walk about. The horses at their pickets were standing in a pond; the

deep dry nullahs were transformed into rushing
rivers; the 95th, who had established their cooking
places in one of them, had not only their dinners but
their cooking vessels carried away.   A piece of un-
dulating ground in front of the Horse Artillery lines
became so full of water that the men began to bathe,
and a bheestie's bullock had to swim across.   Enormous green frogs suddenly appeared, and in such
numbers that their croaking kept me awake the
greater part of the night.   But the most severe annoy-
ances connected with this deluge were the winged
ants, which appeared as soon as the lamps were
lighted on the first evening of the rains; the light
had no sooner been brought than it was obscured and
nearly extinguished by these insects, which came
in whole hordes at once.   At first, dinner and the
ants seemed incompatible; but an officer who had
served for some years in India suggested the removal
of the lamp to the farthest corner of the tent, where
it was placed upon the floor; the ants, following the
light, clustered and buzzed round it, leaving us to eat
in darkness certainly—but in peace.   The next day
there was a renewal of the heavy rain, after
which the sky cleared, and no more fell for a
fortnight.

Sir Hugh Rose's despatch, forwarded as early as
possible after the evacuation of the city, appeared in
some of the local papers.   It was written for the
telegraph, and was necessarily concise :—

" Gwalior " (so it ran) " taken, after a general action of five hours and a half."

" The Ranee of Jhansi killed."

Now as this message was worded, the whole of the fighting on the 17th was ignored. Although there can be no doubt that the easy afternoon's raid on the 19th was attributable to the lesson taught the rebels by Brigadier Smith's force on the 17th. They were also concentrated by being driven in from the heights, and so became an easier prey when attacked by Sir Hugh Rose, in conjunction with Smith's brigade, on the 19th.

Two messengers had been despatched to Sir Hugh Rose on the 17th, during the action, but no assistance was sent; and we heard afterwards that the division could not account for the heavy firing which they heard, but concluded it was *the mutineers quarrelling amongst themselves!*

With regard to the Ranee of Jhansi, nothing is known with certainty, except that she was killed. Various stories got afloat; amongst others, that she was run through the body by a private of the 8th Hussars, who, as she was dressed as a man in a white turban and crimson tunic and trowsers, had no idea that his sword was pointed at the breast of a woman. Another story had it that she died, not from a sword-thrust, but from two shot wounds. Sir Hugh Rose told me, that although mortally wounded she was not actually killed on the field, but was carried off the ground, and ordered a funeral pile to be built, which she ascended and fired with her own hand while almost in the act of dying; an instance of fierce and desperate courage that I can only listen to with wonder. At all events, on the 17th of June her restless and intriguing spirit passed away: a subject of regret perhaps to those who admired her energy and courage, but of congratulation to all who are concerned in endeavouring to settle the intricate and disturbed affairs of this unhappy country.

L

## CHAPTER X.

" The fated hour is come—the hour whose voice
  Pealing into the arch of night must strike
  These palaces with ominous totterings,
  And rock their marbles to the corner-stone."

                                        BYRON.

WHILE we were in camp before Gwalior news
reached us that the eyes of another of England's
best and bravest had closed in death. Sir William
Peel, the Bayard of our modern chivalry, who
risked his life so freely in the batteries before Sebastopol, and had so many hairbreadth escapes, that he
used to say, " the bullet was not cast which was to
kill him ; " after distinguishing himself as nobly in
India, has fallen a victim to smallpox.

Although we had changed our ground, the purer
air brought no alleviation of my husband's suffering;
nor did it raise me from the mental and physical
prostration which overwhelmed me. The kindness
of the Brigadier induced him to think the situation
of our tent not sufficiently healthy, so he procured
for us an introduction to Major Macpherson, the
political agent at Gwalior, who, with that princely

hospitality which is, I suppose, only to be met with
In India, immediately placed a suite of rooms at our
disposal in the part of the Maharajah's palace in
which he resided.

The Maharajah's palace, when I first saw it, suggested two ideas: the first was an Italian palazzo;
the second, a feudal castle. Its graceful arches,
pillars, and flat-roofed verandahs, rise round three
sides of a large square. Windows it has none, the
interior being screened from the sun by crimson
satin purdahs trimmed with gold. Large tatties of
camel thorn fill some of the spaces between the
pillars, and as they are kept constantly wetted by
men employed solely to dash water against them, they
cause the hot air which passes through them to become of a refreshing coolness. Natives in white robes,
with turbans of crimson or green, flitted through
the inner archways or sat upon the flat roofs of the
verandahs; while in the square or yard of the palace
eighty horses were picketed, and the armed retainers
waited, ready at a moment's call. Separated by a
small garden from the principal building is another
palace, set apart for the occupation of the Political
Resident, since the frightful mutiny of 1857 destroyed his house and every vestige of his property.

The history of Gwalior, from May 1857 to June
1858, has been eventful enough. In the month of
April of the former year the Maharajah and his
ministry had reason to fear that an outbreak was

likely to occur; and, in consequence, Major Macpherson caused all the women and children to be withdrawn from the cantonments, and placed in his apartments in the palace; an arrangement which, as the officers of the contingent steadily refused to believe in the approach of danger, was received on the part of the ladies with many complaints and much discontent. The cloud having apparently passed over, the ladies were let out of durance. The large cantonment, which was inhabited by the English officers of the Gwalior Contingent, with their wives and families, extended over miles of ground on either side of the city. There they lived without doubt or suspicion, in the enjoyment of every luxury, and in all the listless indolence that Indian life engenders. To the last moment they would listen to no voice warning them of the disaffection of the troops. Day by day passed on, and as the news of other regiments having mutinied reached them, they continued to assert that " they would trust their men as themselves." Suddenly, even as the flood came in the days of Noah, the hurricane of insurrection burst above their heads. So unexpectedly, indeed, did it come, and so heedless were they, that even when a messenger arrived as they were sitting down to the mess dinner, to tell them that the soldiers were loading the guns, an officer, who went out to see, returned laughing, and treated the whole affair as a jest. Fatal supineness! In less than an hour

some of them had already atoned for their blind-
ness by death.   One or two officers who rushed
out at the first booming of the guns never returned
again.   A lady, watching from a window for her
husband, saw a young lad, whom she knew, fall
pierced by a ball.   With that impulsive courage
which some few women possess, and which lifts
them above heroism, she rushed to the succour of
the wounded youth.   Her little child, ignorant of
danger, toddled after her, and soon child and mother
and the friend she tried to succour, lay in a lifeless
heap together :

> " There did not 'scape the glaive
> Man that frowned, or babe that smiled."

Meantime, by the light of the blazing bungalows,
the survivors, leaving nineteen of their number
beyond the reach of fear and suffering, hastened
away towards Agra, some on horseback, some in
carts, some in carriages, some afoot.   One party
of ladies was taken away by some of the friendly
natives, hidden in a hovel, and sent on afterwards
in a country cart, concealed beneath the goods which
it contained.   But how can I, who, thank God, have
never seen it, hope to convey an idea of these scenes
of murder—of the blazing bungalows and the utter
destruction of property—of the wild flight—the terror
—the despair—and the utter desolation of many a
broken heart.

Well-built and handsome houses, noble palaces,

and lovely gardens, were by the next morning involved
in a common wreck.   The town itself received no
damage.   In the long white street, with its irregular houses, ornamented with screens of fretted
stone, so elaborate as to resemble perforated card-
board, but spoiled and disguised with abominable
whitewash, not a stone was broken or defaced.
The admirable roadway, constructed by the Maharajah, remained entire; and the bridge of minarets,
and mosque of many domes, preserved their solid
and beautiful proportions.

The destruction of the Residency entailed great
loss of property upon our hospitable host; a misfortune which was nearly being repeated when, in
1858, Gwalior again fell under the power of the
rebels, and Scindia was obliged to fly.   As soon as
the Maharajah had withdrawn, the work of plunder-
ing the town began systematically and in earnest.
Scindia, who had spent large sums in English and
French furniture during a recent visit to Calcutta,
returned on the 20th June to find it broken to
atoms.   Fortunately for Major Macpherson, the part
of the palace appropriated to him had been occupied
by Tantia Topee, and was in consequence preserved
from injury, so that the large and massive mirrors,
with their frames of crimson and gold, ornamented
with gilt lions and horses, the sofas, massive arm-
chairs, carpets, chandeliers, and exquisite French
lamps, as well as the numerous pictures which

decorated the walls, remain in their pristine glory.

Now that my energies are dormant and my body weary, I feel as if I could easily accommodate myself to the life of an eastern princess. The cool and lofty rooms, made as dark as possible, the punkahs and cuscuss tatties, and, above all, the wide paved courtyard, which affords abundant space for exercise, seem to me most delightful. I sit leaning against the high carved parapet, in which are open spaces like windows, and ensconced in one of these like a picture in a frame, I look down at my ease upon the gay and idle crowd, which presents numberless objects to attract and amuse a European; that is, so long as he can overlook it without mixing in it. As I watched there one day, I saw the Prime Minister (of whom more anon) on his way to pay a visit of state to Sir Robert Hamilton, the Governor of Central India, who had just arrived at another of the Maharajah's palaces, about a mile out of the town, called the Phool Bagh, or Garden of Flowers. The procession was headed by seven elephants. The first of these "huge earth-shaking beasts" was of unusual size, his housings consisting of a head-piece of crimson velvet, thickly embroidered with massive gold, and edged with deep gold bullion fringe. Two small saddles of black velvet, very like regimental saddles, were on his back, and kept in their places by a crupper, orna-

mented with large round bosses of silver, each as
large and heavy as a small shield. A sonorous bell
hung on either side to give notice of his approach;
an enormous cloth of green velvet covered him
from head to tail; while round his vast neck and
ample throat were six or seven silver chains or necklaces, each big enough to hold a good sized boat
to its moorings. His huge unshapely fetlocks were
adorned with bracelets and anklets, which tinkled
as he walked. In his wake followed six other elephants, all differently caparisoned, but none of them
so gorgeous as the first. After these came the led
horses—the priceless horses of Cattawar. These
animals, in accordance with the ideas of Indian
state, are fattened upon sugar, sheeps' heads, spices,
and all sorts of food, to such excess as to be incapable of any quicker pace than an ambling, shuffling
walk, while their martingales of crimson silk, and the
severe bit, make them arch their necks like a bended
bow. After they had passed, accompanied by a
horde of foot-people, some wealthy man, a diamond
merchant perhaps, followed in a richly decorated
palanquin, escorted by a train of attendants on foot.
Native cavalry soldiers, appointed to patrol the
town, clattered down the street at a canter, regardless of the dogs' toes, or the horns of the sacred
buffaloes which are always wandering about an Indian
town, secure alike from blows or butcher; and in
many cases a great nuisance, as they never trouble

themselves to get out of the way of passers-by. Merchants selling their wares, beggars screaming for alms, pariah dogs, idle soldiers, and ugly women, completed the show.

On the second morning of my residence in the palace I received a notification from the Maharanee, that she wished to have an interview with me on the following day at six A.M. I was the more pleased with the expression of this wish as the Bhae-si-bhae, widow of a former Maharajah, and a woman of very great Indian celebrity, was one of the visitors at the court. The Maharajah ordered an interpretress to be in attendance, and escorted by Major Macpherson, I presented myself at the durbar at the time appointed. After passing the Maharajah's private chapel, and ascending a broad stairway, we came to an upper gallery, branching off into numerous passages, only wide enough to admit of one person passing at a time; they were so constructed for purposes of defence. These finally led us to the durbar hall, one end of which was screened off by a crimson satin purdah, into which were inserted perforated silver plates, which serve to afford the ladies a view of everything passing in the durbar while they themselves remain concealed. Behind this curtain was the reception room of the Maharanee. We arrived early, and after waiting about five minutes were admitted into the presence of the Maharanee, who with three other ladies rose from

their chairs on our entrance. My interpretress
salaamed profoundly and made offerings of gold
pieces, but the ladies extended their hands to me.
The Bhae-si-bhae sat in the place of honour next
the purdah, and arrested my attention at once, both
by the simplicity of her toilette and the great dignity
and self-possession of her deportment. The lustre
of her still glorious eyes reminded me of the light
which shines through port wine when held against
the light. She is over seventy years of age, but
apparently as energetic as in the days of her fiery and
intriguing youth. As little is known of this remark-
able woman at home, I subjoin a brief sketch of her
history :—

" In 1779, when young Scindia had laid Holkar
at his feet, and was keeping the country round
Poona in alarm, arrangements were made for his
marriage with the beauty of the Deccan, daughter of
Shirazee Rao Ghatgay, an important Mahratta Chief
at the Court of the Peishwa. The Maharajah's
proposals were accepted on condition that the bride's
father was to be made Prime Minister. The royal
couple lived happily together. A considerable
family was born to them, of whom two daughters
grew up to womanhood. In 1821 their favourite
daughter died, and her mother was so disconsolate
that she and her husband sought for some considerable time the seclusion of the country. Throughout,
the Bhae-si-bhae has been a woman of great activity

and enterprise, exercising almost unbounded influence over her husband and the ministers of the Court. She was in the habit of going out on horseback with her ladies, delighting in the chase, and amusing herself with the javelin exercise. In March, 1827, Dowlat Rao Scindia died at Gwalior, and leaving no male issue, his widow was permitted to exercise the right of adoption. He had often been urged before his death to adopt an heir, but always postponed doing so, saying he wished that his widow should hold the reins of government.

" Several months after the widow adopted Moodk Rao. He soon showed symptoms of turbulence and cruelty. He naturally expected to be raised to the throne on attaining the proper age, but the Bhae-si-bhae was in no hurry to resign her authority. He attempted to enlist the Governor-General, Lord W. Bentinck, and the Resident on his side, by spreading a report that the regent had attempted to take his life by means of poison. In July, 1834, a revolt took place at Gwalior. One half of the army joined the Bhae-si-bhae, and the other remained faithful to the Maharajah, who had the great majority of popular sympathy on his side. The regent then consented to the instalment of the Maharajah, and leaving the capital took up her residence at Dholpore, accompanied by 6,000 armed men. Military tumults followed, and the Bhae-si-bhae was strongly suspected of intriguing for the recovery of the throne.

She was, therefore, forbidden the capital, and placed in strict sequestration. Shortly after she went to Futtyghur, where she established herself in an indigo factory, her followers being hutted round her. Some months after she was assigned a residence in the Deccan, afterwards altered to Malwa, with an income of six lakhs of rupees annually (60,000*l.*) Her worthless adopted son died in 1843, when another revolution occurred, and the country was finally taken under our closer supervision. The widow of the late chief (Moodk Rao) then adopted the present representative of the house of Scindia, and with his family the Bhae-si-bhae seems to have been staying when the Calpee rebels seized the place on the 1st of June, 1858."

The Maharanee, about eighteen years old, and dressed in black and gold, with sumptuous ornaments, was chiefly interesting on account of her little child, a girl of three years old, laden with pearl ornaments. She herself was almost entirely silent, and the widow of the late Maharajah, whose adopted son now reigns, was equally so; but the old lady and myself kindled into conversation at once, as flint and steel emit fire.

" Was I the Englishwoman who had gone with the armies to make war upon the Ruski?" " She thought I was a much older person." " Could I ride on horseback?" " Had I seen a European battle between the English and the Ruski?" " Ay," she

said, her dark eyes dilating as she spoke, " I, too,
have ridden at a battle : I rode when Wellesley Saib
drove us from the field, with nothing but the saddles
on which we sat."

She made me describe all I saw of the fight on the
19th of June, and asked to see my horses.   Then
suddenly telling me to take off my bracelets, she,
scarcely looking at them, passed them on to the other
ladies, and recommenced her conversation with me.
She showed herself justly proud of the beautiful
palace and town wherein she had lived and reigned
so long.   Presently women appeared, bearing trays
of costly shawls.   " These are presents," whispered
Mrs. Filose, my interpretress, and in the innocence
of my heart, unaccustomed to the polite fictions of
Eastern Courts, I fancied that the costly shawl of
crimson and gold was destined for my future wear.
How gorgeous it would have looked over a white
moire antique !   My surprise was great at being
told merely to take the tray in my hand and pass it
on to a woman who stood in waiting behind my
chair.   Seven times was I thus tantalized, but as
the last tray approached, the Bhae-si-bhae, taking a
piece of fine white Chandaree cambric, gave into my
hands, bidding me " keep it."   Numerous offerings of
fruit, betel-nut, rose-water, sweetmeats, &c., followed;
when my interpretress salaamed, the ladies shook
hands with me, and we withdrew.   The numbers of
women in attendance made the air hot and close.   We

returned to the apartments of the Resident through the lines of horses picketed in the court-yard.

Soon after I had reached my room, I received a note saying that the Maharajah had signified his intention of paying me a visit, and would present himself in half an hour. Punctual to his appointment he came, attended by the Prime Minister and one or two officers of State. The Maharajah cannot be more than thirty years of age: his face is swarthy and dark, with keen, but sensual eyes ; and a mouth expressing intractability and self-will. Nevertheless, he is a good-looking man, dressed in exquisite and most simple taste, and with elaborate care. He was not conversational. He has a slight impediment in his speech, and is shy of speaking before strangers. He was good enough to inquire after my husband's arm, which he carried in a sling, and to say a few grateful and gracious words about the army which had restored him to his kingdom. He expressed great astonishment that a lady should be found (he was good enough to say) of sufficient enterprise and courage to accompany an army in the field, and said he had submitted to the Governor-General and Supreme Council a design for a decoration, which he intended to confer on our troops, and that when it was accepted, he should have much pleasure in conferring upon me a distinction so fairly won. These words raised in me a world of busy thoughts. To have had the Crimean medal almost in my grasp, and not to have possessed it after all, had been a disappointment the keenness and bitterness of which can be suspected only by a few. It is useless now to dwell upon that mortification. If the troops are permitted to wear the Maharajah's decoration, and I should receive it, it will at least prove to me that the Indian Prince knows how to appreciate and how to reward a woman's fortitude.

I have seldom seen a man of greater intelligence and refinement of manners, or one who impressed me so favourably as did the Prime Minister of Gwalior. There was that in his serene, half sad, yet intellectual countenance, which would have made a noble study for Fra Angelica. The face was as spiritual as those of his *confrères* were sensual and earthly.

The morning after these visits, Major Macpherson changed his residence from the Palace, in the Lushkar, to the Phool Bagh, in order to be near Sir Robert Hamilton. Here we had purer air, and a fresh breeze blowing across an open plain through long, wide corridors, shaded by crimson satin purdahs, and cooled by camel-thorn tatties. This residence is more princely than the town palace; it has such wealth of space, with handsome lofty rooms, pillars, fountains, terraces, and gardens of flowers. During the afternoon the Maharajah hearing of my love for horses, with great consideration, sent down his state horses, fully caparisoned for me to see. The one

which he rides on grand occasions is a magnificent
specimen of the Cattawar breed, but so overloaded
with flesh as to appear almost incapable of motion.
He is a deep sorrel chesnut, with two white legs;
his trappings were magnificent.    On his head was a
tall plume of white cock's feathers, fastened into
a jewelled head-stall.    The saddle-cloth was of green
velvet, bound with silver lace.    He had a crimson
velvet crupper, to which were fastened long pendent
draperies falling on either side, and flowing, much as
a habit-skirt would do ; these, with a martingale of
crimson silk, tied as tightly as possible to the nose-
band and saddle-girths, completed his gorgeous cos-
tume.    The bit is one of the most intensely severe I
ever saw, consisting of a string of spurs, or sharp
spikes of iron, the slightest pressure on which draws
blood.    This instrument of torture in his mouth, and
the confined position of his head, made the whole
action of the animal false; and compelled me to pity
as much as I admired him.    Presently our attention was attracted by the sound of a horse approaching from the further end of the terrace, but hidden
by trees.    In a few moments appeared, in all her
self-possessed and calm magnificence, a faultless
thoroughbred English mare.    What a relief it was
for the eye to rest and gaze upon the long lean
head, the delicate, nervous neck, the deep, sloping,
and powerful shoulders, the wide, muscular arms.
To measure the distance from hip to hock, and to

see the genuine English quarters, which beat every Arab in the world for speed. Several other beautiful horses were passed in review; amongst them, the finest and purest bred Arab I had ever seen. How short and sturdy he looked, compared with the length and grace of the English mare; and yet, if not contrasted with her, what a noble fellow he was. I could not but look at the mare shaking the sunlight from her golden chesnut sides, and feel that she spoke to me of home, and that I loved her better than all the Eastern horses, "the Children of the Sun." That evening we drove to Morah, to see the cantonment which had been laid waste in 1857. It was now occupied by Sir Hugh Rose's camp; but the broken walls and smoky ruins stood like spectres among the gay white tents, and told their solemn story in voices without words.

At two o'clock on the following morning, the moon was lighting us on the first of our five marches to Sepree, where we once more hoped to be allowed to remain during the rainy season, and to obtain that rest of which the whole Brigade, both men and horses, stood so greatly in need. In consequence of H. M.'s 95th Regiment being pronounced out of shoes, and in too sickly a state to march, we ert it behind, and it was attached to Brigadier Napier's brigade. About this time the 8th received some small portion of their mess stores which had been despatched from Deesa on camels, under escort of

M

the 71st Regiment. That regiment, being short of
camels, had pressed some of those which it had
undertaken to escort; and the loads of the animals
thus taken had been consigned to the soldiers, who
had emptied twenty-four bottles out of one three-
dozen case of brandy, besides drinking part of the
contents of several others. With a consignment of
wine at Cambay, regimental stores at Nusseerabad,
and others somewhere between Bombay and Mhow,
we are in want of everything. We heard of our
carts being pressed, and of our bullocks being looted
on the road; but when the rains began, and the
black cotton soil became impassable, the remains of
our stores had not arrived.

# CHAPTER XI.

"Down comes a deluge of sonorous hail,
  And prone descending rain."

THOMSON.

ON the morning of Thursday, the 8th of July,
Brigadier Smith's column marched into Sepree.
This was the second time we had entered Sepree
with the idea that it was to be our resting place.
The first time our stay was of very short duration,
as we were ordered off to Gwalior at a day's notice.
As we now had Sir Robert Hamilton's assurance
that we should not move until after the rains had
subsided sufficiently to make the roads·passable and
the rivers fordable, we felt secure of repose, and
shelter, and comparative comfort, and also ventured
to hope for a restoration to health and strength.
We did not hesitate to take possession of a tolerably large room, situated in what must have been
the back yard of a ruined bungalow. The tottering
walls which came crashing down about our ears
pretty frequently as the rains wore on, gave such
an air of insecurity to the whole building, that few
envied us our habitation. There was a "godown,"
or cook-house, which our principal servants occupied,

M 2

some smaller buildings like pigsties, where the
ghorawallahs made themselves comfortable, and a
pigeon-house for the treasure guard.  The Brigadier
gave up the compound to us, so that we had a garden
and large field, an avenue, and two entrance gates;
and as the large tent was pitched near the house, we
were very comfortably accommodated.  Our horses
were picketed near a deep well of clear water, and
I began to luxuriate in the quiet and the rest.

The artillery occupied the lines formerly in possession of the artillery of the Gwalior Contingent,
and the 10th Native Infantry went to the still habit-
able native lines.  The 8th Hussars were partly
under cover and partly in tents, and the Bombay
Lancers remained under canvas; their officers and
those of the Hussars occupying a large bungalow
which had been left uninjured.

It was pleasant to settle down and fancy we were
going to have a little peace.  I was perfectly helpless, having temporarily lost the use of my right
hand, and felt that unless I was allowed to *sleep*, I
should not last much longer.  I slept all night and
half the day, and for three weeks never had sufficient energy to walk as far as the garden, about
twenty yards from the bungalow.

Sepree is an exceedingly pretty place.  The bungalows, with trees tastefully planted round them,
have almost the appearance of English villas, especially in the rains, which make India as green as

England.  I flattered myself with the hope of
remaining for some time at this delightful spot, and
even went so far as to write to Mhow for mustard
and cress and lettuce seeds, which, very fortunately,
did not arrive.  At this time I was unable to sit up
for more than a few hours daily; and about the 25th
of July, when I was suffering more than ordinary
pain, a Portuguese servant came to me and asked
some question relative to the packing of our things.
" Why do you want to know? "—" Go march to-
morrow morning—Kotah!"  When my husband
returned from transacting business with the Brigadier, he told me it was but too true.  The rebels
were supposed to be in the neighbourhood of Jeypoor,
whither General Roberts was gone, from Nusseerabad, in pursuit, and it was dreaded that they would
establish themselves in the strong fort of Boondee,
or, worse still, in the arsenal at Ajmere.

Brigadier Smith received two imperative orders,
one forwarded by Brigadier-General Napier, and the
other by General Roberts, to join the division under
the latter as soon as possible.  Meanwhile, the
heavens were flushed with lightning, and hard and
steadily came down the rain.  A pleasant prospect
truly, that of marching and encamping in the midst
of the rains of a tropical climate, risking fever, ague,
and rheumatism, when we are all, with scarcely an
exception, exhausted by pain and fatigue!

Upon the discovery of a ghaut impracticable for

guns, the Brigadier resolved not to attempt the
shortest route by Shahabad, but to proceed down the
Trunk road *viâ* Goonah. This arrangement possessed two advantages; in the first place it avoided
the cross country tracks which are at this time
simply impracticable; and in the second, by marching to Goonah we ran a chance of falling in with
some money, of which the brigade was so destitute
that the commissariat officer reported that he could
only move along the Trunk road, where we were
known, as the people on the Shahabad route would
refuse to supply him on credit. I was glad to find
we were to go to Goonah, as my nice horse Prince
was still left there in Captain Mayne's care, and I
should thus have the opportunity of recovering him
without trouble.

On the 30th July we still found ourselves at
Sepree, and as the rains were incessant, there seemed
to be no immediate prospect of leaving it. A few
days before, Sir Robert Hamilton went through on
his way from Gwalior to Indore; his train was three
days passing through Sepree, and very soon after
leaving it, in spite of his elephants, he stuck fast in
the mud. This news we heard with rather more
satisfaction than the misfortunes of our friends generally afford us; for if Sir Robert Hamilton could
not get on with elephants, how could we hope to get
on with camels, which fall down on slippery or
muddy soils and never rise again. He brought us,

under an escort of Meade's Horse, a lakh and a half
of rupees, which replenished our exhausted treasury.
The miserable condition of the camels which conveyed it reminded us of the gaunt specimens of that
animal in the Crimea, and the poor horses too looked
regularly sodden with the wet.

The Brigadier having represented the inefficiency
of our brigade without European infantry, the unfortunate 95th was again detached from Gwalior, and
sent down to us in carts. They were much delayed
*en route* in consequence of rain, and the Brigadier
ordered a bungalow, with two or three large rooms,
to be fitted up as a hospital for them; for he knew
that by the time they reached Sepree they would
require one. Two days after their arrival, as I was
taking a drive in the gharry for the purpose of in-
haling some fresh air, I met my dear Prince walking
up the road, attended by his ghorawallah, who had
brought him from Goonah without an escort.

The Brigadier now received an order to consider
himself as attached to the Gwalior division of the
army. I am not aware if General Roberts knows
that he is shorn of his fair proportions in the shape
of our brigade; but for ourselves it does not much
matter who commands us, as I am thankful to say
the roads are pronounced impracticable.

If the loss of Sir William Peel was so sincerely
regretted by us, how much deeper, because more
personal, was the sorrow that we felt on hearing of

the death of Lieutenant-Colonel Morris, C.B., of the
17th Lancers.  He was one of those rare combina-
tions of true Christian and thorough soldier who raise
and ennoble the profession to which they belong, and
leave behind them a bright example to be followed
by those who come after.  Although so young, he
was a most distinguished officer.  His gallantry at
Balaklava, where he was severely wounded, brought
his name prominently forward; and before that, he
had already acquired fame in Indian warfare.  On
leaving England in October, 1857, he looked forward
to India as a large field for future distinction, and yet
hardly six months after he had landed in Bombay,
all these visions had passed away; his sword was
sheathed, his armour taken off, and his soul—

> " To Him who gave it rose,
> God led it to its long repose,
>   Its glorious rest.
> But though the warrior's sun has set,
> His light shall linger round us yet,
>   Bright, radiant, blest!"

Not long after this the Brigade was engaged in an
unsuccessful attempt to capture Maun Sing, who
had seized the fort of Powree, belonging to our ally
the Gwalior Rajah.  A feudal baron in the dominions
of the latter, and also connected with him by family
ties, Maun Sing, after a great deal of quarrelling and
squabbling, had been portioned off with a certain
number of villages.  But there are some people who
cannot possibly live within their incomes, and avoid

running into debt. Maun Sing appears to have
been one of these unfortunates, and being out of
pocket, he naturally became dissatisfied. He soon
found himself surrounded by many malcontents,
who flattered him and lied to him, until he allowed
them to attach themselves to his train, and so
from a troublesome relation he was transformed
into a formidable foe. We knew he had been
hovering about Sepree for some time, but as he distinctly avowed that his quarrel was not with the
English, but was simply a family disagreement with
the Maharajah, he was allowed to remain unmolested,
until in an evil hour, tired of being wet through in
his tent, he and his retainers ousted a garrison of the
Maharajah's from the Fort of Powree. As soon as
the intelligence of this aggressive movement against
our friend and ally reached the ears of Brigadier
Smith, he determined to start immediately in order
to recover the fort. So one morning, about the 3rd
of August, leaving behind him only a squadron of
the 8th Hussars, another of Lancers, and two field
guns, under the command of Lieutenant LeCocq, he
set off to march eighteen miles along a cross country
track, in the midst of the monsoon. The force
started at nine A.M., and by five P.M. had advanced
about ten miles towards Powree. On reaching the
fort the Brigadier found it so much stronger than
native information had led him to believe, that he was
obliged to sit down before the place and to despatch

a letter to Gwalior for siege guns and mortars, making his force, meanwhile, as comfortable as circumstances would permit. Maun Sing came out of his fortress to an interview with the Brigadier, who told him he was empowered to offer him his life if he would lay down his arms. He answered, " But I shall be a prisoner until my death. Of what advantage will my life then be to me?" He stated again that his quarrel was solely a personal one with the Maharajah, and had the matter rested in the hands of the Brigadier, he might perhaps have been turned into a valuable and grateful ally, having, as he represented, sufficient influence to keep all this part of the country quiet. The interview, however, terminated inauspiciously. It was the time at which the Lancer picket was relieved, and his attendants, seeing horsemen riding towards them, raised a cry of treachery, and fled into the fort— whither Maun Sing followed them in haste. He sent an apology the next morning for entertaining doubts of our honour, but he ventured outside the walls no more, and there was an end to all hopes of an amicable arrangement. Soon afterwards Brigadier Smith was reinforced by some details under Brigadier General Napier, and a siege train of two 18-pounders and two mortars. Entrenchments were dug, and guns were run into position; during which operations Lieutenant Fisher, H. M.'s 95th, was shot through the chest. Unfortunately, as usual, there was a loophole, an impracticable side to the fort, on which the jungle was so impenetrable, and the ground so broken by ravines and nullahs, that it was impossible to place either guns or troops there. Moreover, the fort was large, and the attacking force was small; but, nevertheless, on the 19th of August, so sanguine were our people, that a message was despatched to Sepree for the rest of the 8th Hussars, the two guns, the 95th, and every convalescent from the hospitals; "for," said the messenger, "we have them in a trap, and only want all the hands we can get to come and kill them." Such a message caused no little excitement amongst the few left in charge of our little cantonment. The camp was swept clean by midnight, and only the sick, and amongst them my husband and myself, remained. When morning dawned we followed the little force, so hastily sent for, in imagination, and fancied them nearly arriving at Powree to assist in the work of slaughter; but, as no news could reach us, as far as we knew, until the next day, we resolved to wait philosophically for particulars until then. We were not a little astonished when about five P.M., Lieutenant LeCocq rode past our tent on his way to report *the return of the force*, sent out seventeen hours before, to Colonel Owen, 1st Lancers, left in command. The rebels had fled about the time that the little reinforcement started to cut them up; and so stealthy were their movements, and so well managed their retreat, that nobody knew either the exact time of their leaving or which way they had taken. Consequently, the pursuing party, which was organised as quickly as possible by Sir Robert Napier, started in the opposite direction to that taken by the fugitives; and in the course of the next day word came to Sepree that Maun Sing and 1,500 of his men were at Reyghur, about six miles from us, while the other 1,500 were at Kollaris, about thirteen miles off. This news kept us on the *qui vive*, as what could be easier than to sweep our little cantonment, if they only had sufficient courage to try it? Everything was put in readiness for defence, and then we betook ourselves to sleep, undisturbed by either dreams or realities of rebels.

Meanwhile the left wing of the 8th Hussars, attached to General Roberts' division at Nusseerabad, had not been idle since they left cantonments on the 27th of July, for the purpose of intercepting the rebels hovering about Jeypoor, and keeping them from taking possession of either Boondee or Ajmere. To convey an idea of the pleasures of marching in the rainy season, and also of the work they found to do, and the gallant manner in which they, in conjunction with the rest of the force, did it, I cannot do better than subjoin copies of two letters received about this time from Lieutenant-Colonel Naylor, 8th Hussars, in command of the left wing at Nusseerabad, who was in the field, although only just recovering from severe illness. The first ran as follows:—

*" Two Miles from Mowgaum, July* 31, 1858.

" WE started from Nusseerabad on the 27th of last month towards Jeypoor, for which place the rebels, who were reported to have increased their numbers to about 20,000, were making. They marched to within about sixteen miles of Jeypoor, and finding that we had intercepted them by going to Langaneer, about six miles from the town, they turned southwards towards Tonk. We followed them; and, on approaching Tonk, the General (Roberts) detached a flying column, consisting of about 130 Lancers, 350 Belooches, part of H. M.'s 72nd, the 12th N. I., B troop of Horse Artillery, and ourselves.

" We started at seven P.M. from Goonsee, where we had already arrived that morning; and, after marching all night, during which we heard a great deal of firing at Tonk, we arrived within about five miles of that place about seven o'clock on the following morning.

" The men were becoming so exhausted from the heat, and the artillery horses so wearied, that we were obliged to halt. I never felt anything approaching to the intense sultriness of that day. We lost two of the 8th from sunstroke, which affected them whilst lying in their tents. The rebels, hearing of our approach, immediately bolted with two small guns which they had captured; and we have been following them sometimes by night, sometimes by day, without any chance of catching them. They have nothing to delay them; and can, with ease, travel twice as fast as we. They are mostly mounted; at least, what remain of them, for their numbers are greatly reduced: our continued pursuit has so disheartened them, that all their infantry have left them. At one place our reconnoitring party saw a body of about 500 Budmashes in the hills, who fired at them and killed a horse. They were supposed to be returning to their homes at Kotah; but the country is full of these fellows, and any camel of ours that cannot get on is immediately looted; and one of our men, when only about half a mile from camp, was fired at, the ball going through the peak of his cap, and grazing his eyebrow. We hear that there are ˉnot above three or four thousand of them left together, and their only object is to plunder towns. We have saved Jeypoor, Tonk, and Boondee, as well as several smaller places, from their depredations. We went through Boondee, and hearing that the rebels had gone through a pass further south, with the intention of endeavouring, if possible, to push on towards Adeypoor, where they have many friends, we made for Jehazpoor to cut them off. . . . . We arrived at this place (Mowgaum) on the 21st; and we have just progressed two miles in eleven days! On arriving at the river we found it was not fordable; but, after waiting three days, succeeded in crossing it.

" The following morning we attempted to march to Etonda; but, after passing through a deep nullah, and floundering along a road always up to our horses' knees, and many times up to their girths in black mud, the day broke, and disclosed to us the pleasing facts that we had progressed about a mile from the camp, and that the greater part of our force, and all our baggage, had been unable to cross the nullah, in consequence of a sudden rise in the water, already sufficiently deep; so we returned to camp; the greater number of us, who were already over, having to wait some hours before the nullah was sufficiently fordable to recross. Since that day we have been unable to move, and have narrowly escaped starvation; we consumed our last morsel of flour on the evening of the 29th, and the horses, who were standing very nearly up to their knees in water, had not had any grain or hay for two days, so it became a most distressing matter of necessity that we should get out of that somehow. Fortunately the rain, which had been pouring for some days, ceased, and enabled us to cross the nullah and get through about two miles of deep mud to a village where we are now encamped. We had to employ *all the camels of the force* to carry the baggage of the Lancers and ourselves. They took over five hours doing the two miles: this was yesterday morning, and we returned the camels to bring up the rest of the force; but as they have not yet arrived, and it is late, I fancy they must have got into a fix. It is quite impossible to get the guns through the two miles we travelled yesterday. The camels suffer terribly in this muddy weather, as they slip down, with their great spongy feet, and cannot get up again. The river by which we are encamped, and which was not more than a small brook when we first arrived, became, when it rained, such a torrent, and ran with such violence, that it resembled a very heavy sea running, and one night was very nearly inundating the whole camp. I had to shift my tent once at midnight, as the river flooded me out, so I moved to a most attractive spot, where the water was only ankle deep instead of reaching to my knees. We have been out of beer and every other luxury for some time, and have to content ourselves with rations, and be thankful that we are not starved. . . . . We hear the rebels are at Mandulgurh, and are anxious to cross the Burnass River to Adeypoor; however, they cannot manage that yet, as the river is not fordable, and as the General (Roberts) is moving along the other bank, I suspect they will have to return to the Chumbul. They have, ever since we have been following them, stuck closely to the hills, never being above three miles from them, in case of being obliged to halt. We hear they are in great distress, and starving in numbers; the late weather must have told most fearfully upon them; I suppose they have been in the villages in the hills near Mandulghur.

As long as they remain where they are neither cavalry nor artillery will be of much use against them."

Englishmen, however, are not easily diverted from their purpose, and a second letter received some time later, gives the result of all these troublesome marches and privations.

"*Neemuch, August* 21, 1858.

". . . . We have had terribly hard work lately. On the 8th of the month we got the order to join General Roberts' force : we had been marching in the morning, but started at half-past six in the evening, and arrived at Bheelwarra about one o'clock the following day, having marched upwards of thirty miles. We then made three long marches—one of nineteen miles, one of twenty miles, and one of twenty-eight miles.

" The following day we were rewarded for our toils, by finding the enemy drawn up and waiting for us, after we had marched about seven miles. We certainly have done what no other column has, in bringing an unwilling combatant to an engagement. We had been following them up closely for seven weeks, when they became so harassed and desperate, that they determined to fight. We found them drawn up in a magnificent position on one bank of the river, with steep hills down to the water. We, who were on the other bank, had to advance down a gentle slope, about a mile long ; the Horse Artillery·

N

and Cavalry moving rapidly down to the bank of the river, where the artillery came into action, but with little effect, as the enemy's guns and troops were concealed amongst the hills; whilst we were exposed to the fire of four guns, three six-pounders and a nine-pounder, at five hundred yards range, until the infantry could get down the hill. The firing on the part of the rebels was at first very bad; but soon after, they got our range and direction perfectly. I moved the cavalry twice a few yards, when I found they were firing accurately; but they continued their fire on us, dropping their shot just at our horses' feet. Two shot went through the ranks without touching anybody, but we lost four horses, and my dear little gentle white horse was struck full in the chest by a round shot. I had just time to jump off him before he fell. We then crossed the river in line, and went up the hill, when the rebels ran away, leaving their guns and bullocks in our hands. The cavalry immediately went after them; and we had a grand gallop of about three miles through the thick of them, as they were running along a road to a village. Their cavalry, which, with few exceptions, were well on a-head, formed on a hill. Having pretty well pumped our horses, I thought it advisable to stop until the artillery and infantry came up. By the time they arrived the cavalry had cut up all the stragglers about the plain, and the infantry had disposed of about two hundred

rebels who were established on a hill round which
we had passed, and from which they had fired at us
as we galloped by.   However, they made very bad
shots: poor Sergeant-Major Holland was killed there,
but no other person touched.   I was then sent on
after the enemy with cavalry and Horse Artillery,
but had to leave the artillery after about eight miles,
as they could not get on.   We then went about seven
miles further, and caught them on the march.   As
we galloped up to them they fired on us, threw
away their arms, and bolted into the jungle.   We
skirmished through it, shooting an enormous number
of rebels, who tried to conceal themselves in bushes.
Very few attempted to make any resistance, as they
had thrown away or concealed their arms.   We took
three elephants and a lot of camels, carrying the
Nawab's kit, containing gold shawls, valued at
10,000 rupees.   We then, our horses being completely exhausted, returned to the General, and
arrived at eleven at night, having been in our saddles since daylight.   We must have ridden a long
distance.   The rebels had in the morning, I should
say, about nine or ten thousand men; there must
have been about nine hundred killed, and they are
now all scattered.   We saw some of their cavalry,
but beyond firing their carbines at a respectful distance, they showed no desire to fight.   The Nawab
and Tantia Topee are supposed to be with about
seven hundred cavalry, endeavouring to cross the

river Chumbul, near Rampoora. I thought that day would, perhaps, terminate our labours; but during the last week we have been so hardly worked that we are brought to a stand-still, men and horses being completely exhausted. I have ceased to count marches by miles, as we generally march with infantry, and they delay us so much on the road, that I calculate by hours. We marched with the General on Monday and Tuesday, and then started at three A.M., on Wednesday, for Gangapoor, arriving there at eleven A.M. We started to join Brigadier Parkes. at eight P.M., and arrived at Chittore, about four P.M. On Friday morning, we started at six A.M. *viâ* Jawud to Neemuch, where we arrived at ten o'clock at night, doing about four ordinary marches in one. Brigadier Parkes wanted to take us out early this morning *thirty-two* miles; but I told him it was impossible that we could get our horses to drag their slow length over more than ten miles. Without our detachment, the Brigadier had a stronger force of cavalry than we have had to pursue their entire army. I shall be glad to hear they have crossed the Chumbul. . . . . . We left Stourton with General Roberts' force, sick with fever. We are all more or less shaky, but I hope rest and beer will set us right. Richards and Haynes are both quite unfit to be with us from illness. . . . . . The name of the place, where we fell in with the rebels, is Kuttoria."

But to return to ourselves, the pursuing column,

which I mentioned as having been organized by Sir
Robert Napier to pursue the fugitives from Powree,
consisted of one squadron of H. M.'s 8th Hussars,
two six-pound guns of the 3rd Troop Horse Artillery under Lieutenant Hoskins, two nine-pound
guns under command of Lieutenant Strutt, some of
Meade's Horse, one hundred of H. M.'s 95th, and
the 10th and 25th Native Infantry; the whole under
command of Lieutenant-Colonel Robertson, 25th
Native Infantry. Before leaving Powree, Colonel
Robertson expressed his intention of not returning
until he had accounted for those, of whom he was
sent in pursuit. The remainder of the brigade
dropped into Sepree by degrees. They were detained some days for want of camels, as between three
and four hundred extra ones were sent with Colonel
Robertson, in order to mount the infantry; and of
four hundred others sent out to Powree, two hundred
went astray, and were not recovered for some days.
At this stage of the proceedings our bandmaster,
Herr König, sent in his resignation, and by way of
making sure, started from Bombay in a sailing vessel
bound to Liverpool, before it was accepted. His
reasons, amongst others, were that "his hair was
turning grey from the climate, and that the Dhobies
had hammered his wife's linen until it was utterly
destroyed." In short, he declared that it was impossible he could remain longer in "so detestable a
country."

It was on the morning of the 31st August that Brigadier Smith marched into Sepree; and the troops which accompanied him had scarcely breakfasted in their newly-pitched tents, when a telegraphic message came in from Jubra-Pattun, saying that the rebels were in possession of the town.  The first idea conveyed by the news was that *we* were to start off without delay to Jubra-Pattun, which is six marches from Kotah.  We were only kept in suspense for a day or two, and then Sir Robert Napier, who had no idea of giving us any more rest or peace, and who seems to have arrived at Sepree with a prejudice against the place, again marched us out.

# CHAPTER XII.

"Faint but pursuing."

"How dull it is to pause—to make an end—
To rust unburnished—not to live in use;
As tho' to breathe were life!"

ULYSSES.

ON the 3rd September the force, accompanied by
the siege train, marched out of Sepree about six
miles, and encamped at Syssee, a village with an old-
fashioned fort, half way to Kollariss. The rain did
not permit us to start before half-past two in the
afternoon, and our tents were not pitched on the new
ground before dark. In the midst of ʻthe night the
Brigadier was aroused by the arrival of a despatch
from Sir R. Napier, who himself remained behind
at Sepree, saying that Maun Sing was again at Rajghur, and requesting that we would detach a force
in pursuit. The Lancers, under Lieutenant-Colonel
Curtis, and the unfortunate 95th, started accordingly
at daybreak, and returned next night, having seen
nothing of Maun Sing, but having marched thirty-
four miles.

The company of the 95th that left in the morning,

piled only sixteen stand of arms on their return; the rest of the men, having fallen out by the way, came lagging and straggling into camp in the course of the night. We were detained for eleven days at Syssee, and it was only on the 7th September that news reached us of the column under Lieutenant-Colonel Robertson, which had started from Powree in pursuit of Maun Sing. After many difficulties and disappointments, after incessant marching and terrible fatigue, they at length overtook the rebels at Beejapore. Major Chetwode, who wrote, reported nine cases of jungle fever. He also stated that Lieutenant Fawsett, 95th, was killed, and Captain Poore and Lieutenant Hanbury, of 8th Hussars, wounded.

The next rumour relative to the movements of the rebels which reached our camp, was one which ultimately affected us very considerably. It was that Tantia Topee had again assembled a numerous force at Bhopal, and was endeavouring to get southwards. At the same time we had a visit from Sir R. Napier, who alarmed us by saying that as the Gwalior and Jhansi troops were not to be disturbed, he intended to make us into *a moveable column* as soon as sufficient camels could be procured from Agra to enable us to move easily and to mount the infantry if required. Soon afterwards we heard that we were to march to Goonah, then that we were to remain where we were, in order to protect Sepree and Kollariss; and, at last, hopes were raised by Sir Robert Napier that we should work our way northwards, and replace the 9th Lancers at Umballah, a hill station about sixty miles from Simla, in a most healthy and delightful climate. But the trumpeters of the brigade by sounding " orders " late in the evening of the 14th September, put to flight all our anticipations of Umballah, on the road to which we should have again passed through beautiful Gwalior, and have seen the famous Taj at Agra, that most wonderful and beautiful tomb, in itself a commendatory epitaph.

We learned that the Brigadier-General had received orders by telegraph from Sir Colin Campbell —now elevated to the peerage by the title of Lord Clyde—to send our unfortunate brigade to Goonah, without loss of time. This order upset all Sir Robert Napier's previous arrangements, and was received with dissatisfaction by us, but with pleasure by the 3rd troop Bombay Horse Artillery, who looked forward to returning to their own presidency. The siege train was taken from us at dawn, and ordered to return to Sepree. I was quite sorry when the elephants went; for being an invalid, and unable to use my foot, it was a great pleasure and entertainment to watch the odd ways and customs of these great beasts. They would dress themselves up like King Lear, in grass and straws, throwing great wisps over their heads and backs to keep away

the flies.   They would then take another wisp and
twist it about until it was properly shaped, when they
would use it as a brush to drive away the same
tormentors from their chests and legs, their great
ears flapping like punkahs all the while.   It was
curious to see the elephant walking to the well,
carrying his own bucket and rope, and making a
staircase of his fore-leg, in order that the mahout
might mount by it.   He first raised the foot a little,
bending the fetlock ; when the mahout had raised
himself upon this, the animal gradually bent his
knee until the man could step easily from the foot
to the fore-arm, and thence scramble up by his ears.
After reading the account of Mademoiselle Djek,
in Charles Reade's " Cream," I have not been
so anxious to trust myself within range of their
trunks ; but they appeared perfectly docile and
were generally trumpeting—a sign of satisfaction I
believe.

On the same morning that the order arrived for
us to move, the 14th September, we had sent all our
sick into Sepree ; and had also despatched thirty
carts, and as many camels, to bring up more than
one hundred sick men from Colonel Robertson's little
column.   These carts, in consequence of our sudden
movements, were recalled.

On the 14th and 15th of September thirteen cases
of fever occurred in the squadron of the 8th Hussars
only.   We now heard that the rebels were not at

Bhopal, but were endeavouring to reach that place; that General Mitchel had sent out his division in three columns; and that we were to march, by a route of sixteen marches, to Bhopal, joining some of General Mitchel's force by the way.

We left Syssee the day we received our orders and marched thirteen miles to Lukwassa, where we were compelled to halt, on account of the rain. It came down as soon as the column reached the ground, and before the arrival of the baggage. The ground on which our tents were to be pitched was soon flooded. The baggage had a weary time of it, some of the carts, which started at three A.M., not arriving until five or six o'clock in the afternoon. The treasure tumbril of the 95th regiment, which had very high wheels, stuck fast in a hole opposite our tent. The pair of bullocks attached to it were utterly unable to move it, and as the blows fell a great deal faster than we liked, my husband sent a pair of powerful bullocks, used as leaders in one of the brigade treasure tumbrils, to assist. Even with this reinforcement, the wheel, which had now sunk nearly to the axle, refused to stir. Several men applied their shoulders to it, while others pushed behind, but with no better success. Eventually, with the aid of another pair of magnificent bullocks, it was hauled out by sheer strength, the leaders pulling until they fell in the black mud. As soon as it was set in motion, the brigade treasure bullocks were detached and the tumbril started again with its own pair; they went on for about twenty yards, and then stuck fast once more.  One of the mess store carts did not come in until the following morning, when five extra pairs of bullocks were required to draw it to the camp.  At this time I received the following letter from an officer of the 8th Hussars, with the squadron in pursuit, under Lieutenant-Colonel Robertson, giving the following account of the action at Beejapore, which appears to reflect the highest credit both upon Lieutenant-Colonel Robertson for the energy and perseverance with which he followed the enemy, and upon the men who fought so well after such great fatigue.

*Goonah, September* 14, 1858.

"We got over more than twenty miles the first day, and luckily hit on the track of those of whom we were in pursuit, at the village where we halted at dark.  We were obliged to march almost entirely by daylight, on account of the rocky and otherwise dangerous nature of the ground, especially on account of the guns.  We followed the track of the fugitives for five marches; and once were so close upon them, that we lighted our pipes at the fires of their encamping ground the night before.  After making five marches we arrived at a village called Sangie, on the banks of a river running into the Parbuttee.  At this place we halted one day, partly on account of having lost all trace of the rebels, and partly because our own horses, and those of the Horse Artillery urgently required rest. At Sangie it appeared that we had lost all trace of Maun Sing,* but that we were on the track of a number of the Gwalior Contingent and others. Our sixth march was not much more than twelve miles. The next day we started late, and did not get to our ground until after dark. Here Colonel Robertson got such information as induced him to think that, by pushing on with a part of his force, he might come up with the rebels. Accordingly, he started at two in the morning with fifty of our men, the Irregulars, the European infantry, and part of the native. The remainder of the force he left with the guns, it being thought unsafe to leave them without protection, as Maun Sing was believed to be in our rear with 1,400 men. Those left behind followed at daylight; and, after a very long march, which took us right out of the jungle into the open country, we came up with Robertson (who had seen nothing of the rebels), and halted under the trees at the same place that we encamped in May last. The Colonel seemed much disheartened, but resolved to make one more effort, and if that did not succeed, promised us to give up the pursuit. The horses were very much done indeed, and most of those

---

* He had doubled back to Rajghur and Kollariss, near Seprce.

of the artillery were without shoes.   After the men
had had their dinners, about five P.M., the same party
started in advance as before, leaving the rest to
follow at daylight.

" To the surprise of many, just at daylight the following morning the enemy were discovered.   They
were encamped on a rising ground, just beyond the
village of Beejapore.   A broad, shallow river ran
past the village, and close to the ground on which
the rebels were.   At a short distance before arriving
at the village, the infantry were extended in skirmishing order along the valley of the river, and the
cavalry were sent round at a trot on the far side
through the village.   The infantry first attracted the
attention of the enemy, but being hidden by the
houses, our fellows, and the rest of the cavalry,
were upon them before they were aware of their
approach, and in the thick of them before they had
time to fire more than one round from their muskets
which they had prepared for the infantry.   They
were completely taken by surprise.   Down the bank
and into the river they went as quick as ever they
could, the mounted men being the first in, but not
without leaving a good many with unmistakeable
tokens of the will with which our fellows handled
their swords.   The infantry caught them as they
crossed the river, but at a great disadvantage, as
the rising sun was full in their eyes.   After the first
dash of our fellows, the work of destruction appears

to have been carried on in a desultory sort of manner. The bank of the river was too perpendicular to allow of horses crossing immediately; they had to ride alongside it a little distance, and cross lower down. They then formed again, and went at the rebels, who were in a body; but from the ground being cut up by deep nullahs and rents, the fight was necessarily of a very scattered character. The enemy ran into the nullahs, and were shot down by dozens, and in some places by twenties. Many fought desperately; being driven to bay, as it were, they could not help it. One man in particular, although brought down to a sitting position, fought until the very last. They fired their muskets, then drew their swords, and stood, until they were either riddled by bullets or pierced by the bayonet. Our casualties, considering the desperate nature of their resistance, were very few; and some of these were caused by accidents from our own people. Poor Fawcett, 95th, was shot high up in the middle of the chest; he breathed for twenty minutes. He and a few men were making a rush at a lot of fellows. Poore (8th Hussars) received a cut on the wrist, severing the tendons, and he is not going on well I am sorry to say, as it will not heal. Hanbury (8th Hussars) got a slice from a sword on the fleshy part of the shoulder and back of his arm. The enemy were all regular sepoys; most of them wore pouches and belts. The greater part had percussion muskets; and several

had medals for Mooltan, Cabul, Pegu, &c. Their
loss must have been nearly five hundred, and few
could have got away without a mark of some sort.
. . . . . The 95th did the greater part of the
work. The 86th were altogether too late, although
they were mounted, while —— made the 95th
march. The 10th Native Infantry worked right
well, and kept up side by side with the 95th, and
never stopped for anything. Sergeant Major Champion is going on well; he was shot in the breast. . . .
Tantia Topee is, as of course you know, expected
to cross the road and go to Bhopal. . . . . The
country we marched through was very like parts
of Herefordshire, wood and rock, with here and
there an opening; and the atmosphere was that
of a forcing house—so hot, steaming, and damp."

This was a brilliant day's work, of which Colonel
Robertson had reason to be proud.

We marched into Goonah at about six o'clock on
the morning of the 21st, and found two pieces of
good fortune awaiting us, viz., our letters and two
tattoos, laden with stores from Mhow, consisting of
beer, sherry, brandy, coffee, writing-paper, &c., all
much needed, and most acceptable. The contents of
the mail was rather amusing, as regarded the Brigadier. About an hour after we had started on our
march in the morning, a messenger from Sir Robert
Napier had overtaken him, saying that the rebels

were all gone to Shahabad, and ordering him to
return and proceed to that place.  As we could only
arrive at Shahabad by retracing our march along
the Trunk Road to within twelve miles of Sepree,
this was disheartening enough.  The mail-bag, however, brought the Brigadier a letter from General
Roberts, desiring that, as soon as he had finished
co-operating with General Michel, he should return
to Rajpootana, and place himself again under General
Roberts's orders.  It also brought a telegraph from
General Michel, desiring him to march immediately
on Seronge, a fortified town, situated south-east of
Goonah, where Tantia Topee has established himself.
So that in about three hours, the Brigadier received
as many different orders from as many different
authorities, and to crown all, the telegraphic wire
was discovered to be broken in two places, so that he
could communicate with none of them.  Sir Robert
Napier would have us march due north, General
Roberts wanted us almost due west, and General
Michel urgently required us south-east!  The hopes
of the Brigade were fixed on joining General Michel,
and the wish to proceed to Bhopal *viâ* Seronge was
universal.

It was fortunate for us that we reached Goonah
before the rains, which again came down in torrents,
accompanied by blinding lightning and deafening
thunder.  These are supposed to be the finishing
rains of the season; and the hard gravelly soil of

o

Goonah enables us to trench our tent sufficiently
to keep it tolerably dry.

On the morning of the 23rd, Brigadier Smith
received a communication from Major Macpherson,
insisting that the rebels were moving on Shahabad.
We ought to feel flattered at the anxiety evinced to
retain the force in Bengal; and might do so, did we
not know that we are only required to act as a police
force, while the Jhansi and Gwalior troops remain
undisturbed. We found Colonel Robertson very ill
at Goonah; and his brigade, the command of which
had devolved on Major Chetwode, 8th Hussars,
absent in pursuit of some rebels supposed to be passing about forty miles to the south. The morning
after we marched in, the Brigadier received a despatch from Major Chetwode, saying that the information had proved entirely false, and that no rebels
had ever been in the neighbourhood. Major Chetwode then endeavoured to rejoin the Brigadier at
Goonah, but was much impeded by the torrents of
rain. Captain Mayne had been absent with his body
of Irregular Horse for some time, moving south of
Ragooghur. We were detained for three days at
Goonah, waiting for definite orders as to which
superior was to be obeyed; and I was not sorry
to be able to ride round the cantonment now that
it was dressed in green. The tall, mowing grass
rose to our horse's girths, and the thick tangled
bushes, all a-gleam with recent rain, looked more

English and home-like than anything I had seen in
this country.

On the 25th September, at three A.M., we marched
out of Goonah, leaving Captain Poore suffering from
the effects of fever, in addition to his wound, which
was going on anything but well, and taking with us
Sergeant-Major Champion, whose gallant bearing
during the action of Beejapore deserves record.  He
was, as before mentioned, shot through the breast,
the ball coming out beneath the shoulder-blade.  He
naturally believed himself mortally wounded; and
although struck quite at the beginning of the fight,
he continued to ride on and to fight, not knowing
but that each movement of his body might cause
death.  On the first hasty medical inspection, it was
thought that the ball had actually pierced the lungs,
nor was it until after a second and very careful
examination that it was found to have traversed
round the ribs.

The Assistant Quartermaster-General attached to
the brigade having recomoitred the road to Bhadore,
pronounced it totally impracticable; and we, in consequence, took a shorter route for the first three or
four miles.  We marched until daylight through a
fen, full of holes and standing water, with long rank
grass brushing the horses' sides.  I had intended
riding, but went the first half of the march in a
dooley, nor was I sorry to find myself in it, as the
troop horses stumbled and floundered along, sinking

to their knees, and, in the effort to struggle out, falling almost on their heads. I looked out just in time to see "the Pearl," who was saddled and led after my dooley by his syce, go headforemost down a piece of rotten ground into a sedgy hole full of water, after which I closed the purdah, and looked out no more. At length we gained a gravelly soil, and the latter part of the march was pleasant enough. The country was thickly wooded and hilly, with long grass and flowers; and the scenery was really picturesque and pleasing; a luxury one is rarely blest with in India.

The baggage, as might be expected, was arriving by instalments until six in the afternoon; and the next morning, the deaths of nineteen camels, which had been overloaded and had fallen during the march, were reported to the commissariat officer. The rain, which came down steadily that night and the next morning, again stopped us; and we now heard that Tantia Topee and a large force were awaiting us at Seronge. Sir Robert Hamilton reported their numbers at 10,000; and from other, but I should imagine less authentic sources, the Brigadier was informed that they mustered 17,000 men. Our brigade, reinforced by taking back most of our own men from Colonel Robertson, who gave them up unwillingly enough, numbered about 1,100. The odds are great; but no one feels any doubt about our being quite able to cope with them, especially

should Brigadier Parkes and General Michel move
up to help us.   The 17th Lancers are at last turned
out of their comfortable bungalows at Kirkee, and in
squadrons and wings are marching up to Mhow.   Sir
William Gordon, with one squadron, arrived there
some time ago; and Lieutenant Wood, weary of
inactivity when real work was going forward, volun-
teered to serve with the 3rd Bombay Light Cavalry,
and is under Captain Mayne's orders.

On the 27th September, another letter was received from Sir Robert Hamilton, urging the Brigadier to hasten to Seronge.   In vain did he, in his
anxiety to obey the summons, ride down the road
twice before twelve o'clock to see whether he could
not persuade himself that it was passable.   But the
rain was heavy and frequent; and the baggage
animals failing us so fast, with no possibility of re-
placement, that he was obliged to content himself
with fretting and eating out his heart, until three
o'clock in the afternoon of the 28th, when, as the
sun shone and the tents were positively dry, he ventured to try a move of three miles to a piece of red
soil.   He accomplished it, but with severe loss.   I
rode almost the first of the whole column, wisely
remembering that the more the ground was trodden
the deeper it would be.   Presently, the horseman
immediately preceding me sank in the deep black
earth up to the roots of his horse's tail; this was the
first horse down.   He was quickly followed by one

of our own troopers, which was for some time unable to extricate himself, rolling several times over, and being up to his neck. The Horse Artillery had fearful work; nor would they have arrived before the next morning, had not the 95th Regiment assisted them. One horse remained head under for so long that, when first dragged out, he was supposed to be dying. None of the baggage-train, except a few camels, nor the treasure tumbrils, nor the mortars, came in before the next day. Twenty camels were reported " dead," and the road " a wreck of carts." The change, however, was much for the better, as far as the health of the troops was concerned; they were camped on fine, high, dry ground, and no longer laid down to sleep in odorous and slushy mud. A jemadar, of the 1st Lancers, who came in soon after we reached our new ground from spying at Seronge, reported that Tantia Topee had strongly entrenched himself, and that he was aware of Brigadier Smith's approach.

A letter received the following morning from General Michel, announced his intention of making an attack on the south side of Seronge, simultaneously with ours on the north; and added, of course, that " *should the enemy escape, Brigadier Smith's column would pursue.*" But by noon, news had come that the Nana, with a large force, had raised his standard in the north, and that Tantia Topee had abandoned Seronge, for the purpose of

joining him.   The letter suggested that we should
retrace our steps *via* Goonah and Sepree, towards
the Nana; in which case, I may bid a fond farewell
to all hopes of seeing my English box, now on the
road from Bombay to Mhow, and also to the idea of
resting awhile in the latter cantonment.

On the following morning we started at two A.M.,
to march by the large and very pretty fortified
village of Bujianghur into Goonah.   Colonel Robertson, who is still detained here by illness, no sooner
heard of the approach of Brigadier Smith, than he
telegraphed to Sir Robert Napier for leave to resume
the 95th and 10th Native Infantry, but I am happy
to say his application did not succeed.

Our Brigadier, hearing that Tantia Topee and a
large body of men were at Esaughur, started for
that place as fast as the reduced state of the 95th and
the baggage transport would permit.   Captain Mayne
accompanied us with a cavalry brigade, consisting of
his own Irregular Horse and a part of the 3rd Light
Cavalry.   He had joined us the day before, having
come one-and-twenty miles that morning to do so.
On arriving in sight of the town we saw the sky
obscured with smoke.   Not only had Tantia Topee
stormed the place, but he had plundered and utterly
desolated it.   The rear-guard of his force did not
move out until we drew up before it, and a party of
Irregular Cavalry started at once in pursuit.   But, unfortunately, there were two roads from Esaughur in

the same direction, of which the rebels took one, and their pursuers the other. We learnt subsequently that Tantia had actually moved on Mahoulie that day, but as the hearts of all are with the rebels, we can procure no information in time for it to be of use. About this time the most disheartening *contretemps* of our wearisome pursuit occurred. Our Brigadier became aware that Tantia, with 12,000 men, had gone to Chandaree. After anxious deliberation the following plan, the tactics of which are shown by the accompanying map, was resolved upon. Chandaree, as the map indicates, is situated in the vicinity of the Betwa River, which being at that time so swollen as to be absolutely unfordable, was for the moment an insuperable barrier to the escape of the rebels eastward. Lieutenant-Colonel Robertson was ordered to move his force from Goonah to Shahdowra, and so to keep the Western road closed : Brigadier Smith at Esaughur would have defended the Northern and North-western roads; and General Michel was requested to move up from Seronge, in order to prevent the rebels from flying towards the South. A simultaneous attack on three sides, on a given day, with an impassable river on the fourth, seemed to offer the opportunity which had been so long sought for in vain, of putting an end at one blow to the rebel forces in Central India. The only uncertainty as to their utter destruction was the falling of the Betwa, which was not, however, likely to occur in

time to enable them to escape. We waited anxiously
to hear whether General Michel would co-operate in
this well-organized plan, as in his last communication he had declared himself unable to move for
nine days. His Europeans, he said, were out of
groceries, and could not march until they arrived!
Without inspecting the invoice we could not tell
what condiments might be considered necessary to
enable this luxurious force to move, but it was
almost certain that before the nine days were over
the Betwa would be fordable for elephants, and in
places for horses; when Tantia would probably bid
farewell to beautiful, solitary Chandaree, and proceed to possess himself of the rich spoils of Teary.

The guns left by Tantia at Esaughur, nine in
number, were blown up by the Horse Artillery.
The Subar, in charge of the town, who appears
from the number of dead and wounded lying in the
streets to have made as stout a resistance as he
could, was assisted by us with money, as Tantia had
taken good care to leave nothing of any value in the
town. The monsoon by this time, October 7th, had
entirely passed, and the days, once more bright and
cloudless, were of very great heat. Already the
first fresh tinge is off the green, and the country
begins to resume its brown colour. The grass in
the jungle exceeds in height and thickness anything I had ever imagined, and when we first begin
to march in the morning it is saturated with dew,

which makes wading through it like passing through a river; the smell, too, before sunrise is extremely offensive and injurious.

A series of misfortunes befel us at this time, for besides my being a prisoner to my tent and dooley, with a feverish attack which left me so weak as to be incapable of exertion, my pleasant horse " Pearl" was severely kicked on the sinew of the hind leg. There was no prospect of his being able to use his leg for a month, even if lock-jaw did not end his sufferings before that. Sad indeed it was to see his pretty head bowed down by pain, and to watch him limping slowly on three legs, and growing thinner and thinner every day.

On the morning of the 8th of October the detachment of Cavalry, under Captain Mayne, quitted us at Esaughur and marched to co-operate with General Michel. They left in obedience to peremptory orders, thereby obliging Brigadier Smith to call in all his outposts of Irregular Cavalry, which were watching the country between Esaughur and the river, in a northerly direction, and so frustrating all hopes of accomplishing his plan for catching Tantia in a cul-de-sac. I think that were I in a subordinate command in India, I should either throw up the whole thing, and run away in the night, or I should carry out my own plans in the teeth of everybody— coûte qui coûte.

The water of the Betwa, on the 7th of October,

was reported not more than five feet over the ford. From what we heard subsequently, it must in reality have been much deeper. The rebels have with them several elephants laden with treasure. Grain of all kinds is scarce in their wake, as being so flush of money, they have been paying high prices for grain, instead of taking it by force, as is their usual custom. We rode through Esaughur, a mean, but in places a picturesque little town. Its desolation was as complete as that of Chandaree, but it lacked the beauty, which made that place so exquisite in its mourning.

At midnight, on the 9th of October, "boots and saddles" sounded, and by one A.M. the following morning we were again on our travels; halting once more at Mahoulie, which in its dress of tangled green was hardly recognisable. The river, with its overhanging trees, was too thick and muddy to offer a chance of success to the sportsmen, who betook themselves to fishing as soon as the camp business was concluded; the ford was three feet deep, and we were encamped in tall, rank grass and jungle, which we were not sorry to move out of on the following day. Brigade orders were to rouse at two, although the greater part of the baggage carts did not arrive until between five and six the previous evening, and the mortars only came in during the night. It was intended to march to Serai, but despatches received about an hour previous to marching caused Brigadier Smith to direct his course to Monone. We heard that General Michel had come across a portion of the fugitive rebels, and after a fight had killed about two hundred, and taken several guns. Tantia Topee, with 2,500 followers, had escaped over the Betwa—having built boats for the purpose—while the treasure and women were conveyed across on elephants. The urgency of time was so strongly insisted upon by the General, that the propriety of proceeding after the men's breakfasts was discussed, but abandoned on account of the great heat of the sun. The Bheels, who have disturbed the country below Mhow, are reported to have robbed the post; it is certain that no English letters arrived by this mail, although they are known to have been in Bombay by the 28th of September.

Some opinion of the state of the country, and of the tendencies of the people in Central India at this moment may be formed from the contents of the following letter, written by one of a party of three Englishmen travelling down to Bombay on sick leave.

"*Mhow, October 3rd,* 1858.

". . . . Since I started from Sepree I have had as unpleasant a time as any one need desire. You have no doubt heard that when we arrived at Bursode, thirty-one miles from Goonah, we learned that Tantia's advanced guard was at Keelipore, only eighteen miles from our next halting-place—Beora,

on which place he was then advancing, having
ordered 20,000 sirrs of flour and wood to be in
readiness for his army.    As we were struggling
through the mud at the rate of nine miles in twelve
hours, we took the advice of the telegraphic in-
spector, and returned to Goonah, whither he followed
us the next day; and, in doing so, very nearly fell
into the hands of the party whom Colonel Robertson cut off, and who were only five miles distant
from Ragooghur, where we breakfasted. . . . .
We had to remain at Goonah 'chewing the cud
of patience,' as the Persians say, until the 20th,
when we accompanied Major Chetwode to Ragooghur.    We reached Beora, sixty-one miles from
Goonah, in two' days, and were highly elate at the
prospect of a speedy journey to Bombay, when we
were overtaken by one of the severest storms of
thunder and rain I ever remember to have witnessed.    It completely swamped the roads; nor was
it without the utmost difficulty that we reached the
next station of the bullock train, where we arrived
about seven P.M.    The Peon in charge there said
it would be impossible to proceed any further that
night, and advised our remaining in the bullock
sheds until morning, adding, that he would light
a fire for us, and make us as 'khoosh' as possible.
In the morning he proposed to take us by a jungle
path, so that we might avoid the flooded nullahs.
We agreed to this, and proceeded to make ourselves

jolly over a cold fowl and some beer, in spite of the
attacks of numerous hordes of insects, who resented
our intrusion on their domains and vested rights.
Whilst thus making ourselves comfortable under
difficulties, one of our servants called Captain ——
out, and told him we must get away as soon as
possible, as bad work was going on.    Our cook
being sick, did not, like the rest of the servants,
leave the cart, but lay in the bottom of it covered
over with saleetas, and so was concealed from the
notice of the peon, who, leaning against the cart,
thus addressed another man :—

" ' I have made the Saibs khoosh ; and, as soon
as they go to sleep, we can loot the carts.'

" ' But in case they or their servants resist, you
have not enough of men.'

" The peon replied : ' Oh, I have thought of that,
and have sent to the next village for ten or twelve
budmashes who are halting there, and who will do
their business.'

" ' Bohut Atcha ' (very good), replied the other
worthy.

" Our cook, on overhearing all this, was much
alarmed, but remained quiet until one of our servants
went to the cart, when he whispered to him to tell
us directly all he had gathered of this precious plot.
So I sent for the peon, and told him I had changed
my mind, and should proceed at once.    He was
greatly annoyed, and tried to persuade us to remain;

but, seeing we were quite determined, he left us, and went to order the bullocks; and, strangely enough, he and his friend held another consultation close to the same cart.

" ' Those people say they will go on; I have ordered only one pair òf bullocks to each cart, so they will get on slowly enough for you and the budmashes to overtake them.'

" ' But how are we to attack ? '

" ' The drivers will have orders to upset the carts ; you will then manage it easily enough.'

" This being also told me, I insisted upon two pairs of bullocks being furnished to each of the carts as usual, and then told the peon to get into my cart, as I wished for the pleasure of his company down the road. He refused at first, but the muzzle of my pistol applied to his ear, and a gentle *argumentum ad hominem* from the Sergeant Major, induced a speedy compliance. I then armed our ghora-wallahs with swords, and told the peon that if any budmashes came near us I would shoot him that instant, while the ghora-wallahs had instructions to cut down the first driver who upset a cart. You never saw such a face of terror as our friend the peon showed. He whispered a long time with the driver, which I permitted, as I fancied he was giving him instructions to be cautious. Whenever the gharry gave a greater lurch than usual, he exhibited the greatest agitation. So we journeyed to Puchore,

when I gave him over to two of Holkar's sepoys,
who permitted him to escape; but Sir Robert Hamilton has sent people in pursuit of him. We were
detained three days in a filthy native hovel at
Puchore, in consequence of the rising of the river,
which we ultimately crossed on charpoys (native
bedsteads), carried on men's heads. We found that
the Kola Sind River was also unfordable, by which
we were detained another day; and a third river,
the name of which I forget, detained us the greater
part of another; thus, altogether, we had a most
unpleasant journey; we lived in dirty sheds, and
were half starved; a mode of life not very con-
ducive to the restoration of health. We are now
detained at Mhow in consequence of the Bheels
being out on the road, joined by some 200 of
Holkar's Horse. They have broken the telegraphic
wire, looted the dâk with the English mail, seized
the bullocks of the train, and smashed the carts,
so our journey hitherto has not been as fortunate
as adventurous. . . . ."

On the 12th October General Michel rode over
to our camp, which was only nine miles from Mongroulee, where his force was halted, and made
arrangements with the Brigadier for pursuing the
enemy into Bundelcund. It was decided to form
the united forces into three columns, placing cavalry
and light field guns in the centre; the left wing
being composed of Brigadier Smith's infantry, with

100 cavalry, and two light guns, and the right column of General Michel's infantry, under command of Colonel Lockhart. The cavalry, so it was arranged, were to cross the river at a ford near Mongroulee, with between four and five feet of water. · Brigadier Smith was to cross at a ghaut near Chandaree, and Colonel Lockhart somewhat lower down. These three were to form a junction with General Whitelock, at Teary; but no sooner was the plan formed, and the arrangements made, than the rebels were found not to have gone to Teary at all, but to have taken a northerly direction.

On the 14th of October the centre wing, consisting of three troops 8th Hussars, a squadron 17th Lancers, three troops 1st Bombay Lancers, a wing of 3rd Bombay Cavalry, Mayne's Horse and Horse Artillery, marched to a ford on the river Betwa, about thirteen miles from Serai; and as Brigadier Smith had received information that the ghaut at Chandaree was utterly unfordable, he marched his infantry to the same place, hoping to get across. But on the evening of the day on which we arrived, General Michel decided that the river was quite impracticable for infantry and for baggage carts, and ordered Brigadier Smith not to attempt to cross it at all; but to proceed along its left bank as far as Chandaree, from which place he could watch two fords—the one near that town and the other a few miles further down the river.

P

Our little force now consisted only of the Brigadier and staff, H. M.'s 95th, the 10th Native Infantry, one troop of Hussars, two troops of Lancers, and two Horse Artillery guns, with five Sappers and Miners attached, together with the two mortars sent us from Sepree; and on the morning on which General Michel crossed the river, we returned to Serai, not a little pleased that our baggage had escaped being drenched and drowned, and delighted to find ourselves moving independently, as we, ourselves particularly, were thereby relieved from a great deal of worry and annoyance.

We heard at this time of the arrival of Major Seager in Bombay, which, as he is anxious to purchase, may perhaps cause great and, on some accounts, very beneficial changes in the regiment, although, should they involve the loss of Lieutenant-Colonel Naylor, they will cause universal regret.

On the morning of the 17th of October we again pitched our tents amongst the hills that surround Chandaree, where we halted for some days to watch the fords of the Betwa. If the country was beautiful in May, when the trees were leafless and the ground barren and bare, it acquired a double charm now that the earth was green and the trees bent down with foliage, and in many cases with flowers. A beautiful ruin of what had once been a serai or resting-place for travellers, lay on the right of our camp, and before us were the hills topped with the

fortifications that defend the town. This evening
the mail of the 30th August reached the camp, and
a sergeant brought letters to our tent, containing
intelligence of the death of my Crimean companion
and friend, the chesnut horse Bob. When we left
England he had been committed to the care of
friends whose kindness he had enjoyed for nearly
twelve months, and from them we received the following account of his death:—

"I have to tell you of what I fear will give you
pain—poor Bob's sudden death—not by bullet, but
in the common course of nature. He had never had
ache or ailment since he came into our stable, and
on Sunday, 29th August, he took his morning's feed
at eight o'clock, and went out to exercise in the park
as usual. Suddenly he staggered and fell, and was
dead in less than five minutes. He was only being
walked round, the groom riding him, and leading
another horse. He was buried in Park Coppice,
where several other old favourites lie. We are
almost as sorry for his death as you will be; he led
an easy life whilst in our care. 'The 'Squire' very
seldom worked him, and he ranged about in his
large loose box, more a show horse than anything
else; for every one who came to the house was taken
to see him."

The next morning we moved down a steep and
rocky road, which cut the horses' feet very much, to
the east side of Chandaree, nearer the fords, and

encamped on more open ground. Receiving vague intelligence of some Bundealahs on the opposite side of the river, the Brigadier sent a party of the 95th, under command of Major the Hon. E. C. H. Massey, to reconnoitre. It was found that they were encamped and had with them two or three small boats, which were soon after taken by us. They fled as soon as the white faces became visible, although they were on the other side of water between seven and eight feet deep.

We are urgently looking for a reinforcement of camels, as there is actually not a spare camel in the force; and of the few that are left some die daily, while others can hardly carry their loads, owing to the frightful sores on their backs. For these the natives know no remedy but the actual cautery, and one is nearly deafened at times by the roars of the unfortunate victim whose wounds are being comforted by the application of a red-hot iron.

The beautiful comet, which has been visible to us for many nights, is now passing out of sight. Its first appearance was on the evening of the 29th of September, soon after sunset. Since then it has been seen nightly with more or less distinctness. At first it caused a great sensation among the camp followers, who were anxiously inquiring whether it was a star of good or evil omen. For my part I cling to the hope that it will prove the herald of peace if not of good will, and that as its splendour has witnessed the decline, its departure may mark the suppression of the mutiny.

On the evening of the 22nd of October, as we were still resting—four whole days of rest—beneath the shadow of the hills round Chandaree, a native arrived with intelligence that the rebels intended to cross the river at the Rhait Ghaut. As the information was given by a man who had offered himself as a spy, and as nothing was more probable than that the enemy, knowing Scindia's force in Chandaree to be short of ammunition, should endeavour to draw off the European brigade, in order to gain an opportunity of crossing the river at the ford opposite the town, it was decided to wait until the spies of our own camp returned. In the meantime it was intimated to our informant, that if his intelligence proved correct he would be well rewarded, but if on the contrary, he was found to have spoken falsely, he would be hanged, a consummation he appeared to contemplate with the most frigid indifference. Next morning, however, his news was so far confirmed, that the enemy were found to be hovering on the banks of the river, undecided whether to cross or not; and in consequence of orders, which arrived shortly before noon from General Michel, Brigadier Smith marched at three P.M. for Bhorassa, in order to guard that ford, which was only knee-deep. The Brigade reached Serai about half-past nine o'clock in the evening, having marched over a terrible road, up a very steep and rocky ghaut. No tents were pitched, the men laid down in the open air, and by five o'clock the next morning after this sixteen-mile march, were again on the tramp, ten miles further to Mongroulee, where no carts, commissariat or private, appeared until four or five o'clock in the afternoon. The English Infantry had proved themselves more enduring than the native cattle, which were unable, without rest, to accomplish the severe work over the incredibly bad roads. The men lay down until midnight, when reveillée sounded, and the brigade then completed the remaining twenty miles which lay between them and Bhorassa, thus performing a forced march of forty-six miles in forty-two hours.

Enough cannot be said in praise of the endurance and fortitude of the non-commissioned officers, and men of the 95th—I do not include their officers, as they were, I believe without exception, mounted, and so incurred no more fatigue than the cavalry; but when it is considered that on this occasion the regiment accomplished, beneath an Indian sun, a march far beyond anything that ever was required of them in their native country, it becomes a matter of regret that men, so heroic in endurance, should have been so severely tried.

We encamped at the village of Bhorassa on the left bank of the Betwa, opposite the Fort of Koozwye, wherein resides a friendly Begum, who sent her younger brother, the Nawab, accompanied by trays of sweetmeats, to make his salaam to the Brigadier.

Just before we reached the end of the march we heard that General Michel had encountered the rebels, under Tantia Topee, at a place called Sind-waha, on the right bank of the Betwa; and the next day more detailed accounts arrived by dâk, and we learned that on the 19th a severe battle was fought, wherein the enemy mustered about ten to one. They attempted to charge the Horse Artillery guns, but were driven back by the Hussars. Lieutenant Harding, 8th Hussars, was very severely wounded in the right side, Captain Heneage's troop lost eight men killed and wounded, and Captain Penton's troop also suffered loss. A nullah, which ran in front of our men, saved a good many of the enemy, and the broken nature of the ground made it very difficult for cavalry to work. But every account that has as yet reached us agrees in saying that had the cavalry been permitted to pursue as energetically as it was their wish to do, the loss of the enemy would have been far more considerable.

At Bhorassa-Koozwye, we remained four days, spent by the Brigadier and Staff in endeavouring to collect intelligence of the whereabouts of Tantia and his treasure, and by me, in riding about in the vicinity of the camp.

One evening we rode to look at the Betwa, of which so much has been said. We found a wide river, with a bed composed partly of sand and partly of rock. The water had sunk so much that the ford was easily passable on horseback. As we returned we met a wild boar, who like ourselves was taking his exercise in the cool of the day. The broken nature of the ground, and the number of large holes, made it impossible to give him chase, without more danger to our horses and ourselves than the fun of the gallop was worth. In India the ground is in very many places perforated with deep holes, which are never filled even with the mud caused by the rains. Some of them, just large enough to admit a horse's leg, are from two to three feet deep, others are larger and deeper. In places the land is honeycombed with them, so that it is necessary to ascertain the nature of the soil before attempting even a trot. At the same time, the dexterity with which a horse will gallop over ground covered with holes is very wonderful—that is to say, if his rider gives him his head, and lets him trust to his own eyes and feet; should the rider, however, attempt to put his judgment in place of that of his steed, the chances are that he earns a fall, upon ground which for eight months of the year is as hard as brass.

# CHAPTER XIII.

"The two corps of this army, particularly that which has been in the north, are in want of rest. They have been in the field, and almost constantly marching since January last; their clothes and equipments are much worn, and a short period in cantonment would be very useful to them. The cavalry likewise are weak in numbers, and the horses low in condition. I should wish therefore to be able to canton the troops for a short time."

*The Wellington Despatches.*

No communication was received from General Michel from the time of the arrival of the order to move from Chandaree until the 31st October, when a letter reached us at Malaghur, informing us that General Michel, who was now marching south, had, on the 25th inst., come across and dispersed a body of 3,000 rebels. He desired the Brigadier to proceed by easy marches to Seronge. We hear that three lakhs of rupees are at Saugor, awaiting "a strong escort" to be supplied by Brigadier Smith; two lakhs for our own column, and one for that under General Michel.

On the 30th October the 10th Regiment of Native Infantry received a reinforcement of 250 men and four officers, and on the following day the brigade was joined by 500 irregular cavalry, under Captain Buckle.

On the 1st of November we marched to Moundalh, and the day following to Taal. Both these marches were in the direction of Seronge, to which place we were proceeding in order to cover Goonah. General Michel himself had hastened south, and we heard of his force as being near the Nerbudda River. Great diversity of opinion exists as to whether the force under Tantia Topee will cross that river. Crossing the Nerbudda is like crossing the Rhine—the opposite shores are inhabited by people of different race, prejudices, and opinions. Some say that once across the Nerbudda Tantia Topee would meet with very little sympathy or encouragement.

A letter from an officer of the 8th Hussars shows that the cavalry brigade has been well worked in the pursuit. He says :—

" After we left the old brigade we crossed the Betwa River with less difficulty than we expected, and marched for a great distance southward. We met Lockhart's Brigade, and the two went on together in the direction of Teary. The enemy were known to be somewhere in our neighbourhood, but few suspected them to be so near as they afterwards proved. We marched about twelve miles through an open cultivated country, and had forced some little distance ahead of the infantry, when all at once the enemy's picquets were seen galloping in, and in a few moments we came in sight of the whole army, extended in line, on some open ground

near the village of Lindwaha. We went steadily
on, and the enemy fell back upon some ridges, with
fields of very high standing grain towards the centre.
A squadron of 8th Hussars, the 17th Lancers, and
native regular cavalry were on our right; the
Horse Artillery, one troop of 8th, and Mayne's
Horse, went away to the left. We rather hurried
up into action; but I rather think the General was
afraid of their slipping through his fingers. The
action began on the left, by the enemy opening fire
upon us from four guns. We were so short of men
that we could only reply with three. I could not
tell what was doing on our right, on account of the
high grain. After a short cannonade, the enemy,
possibly emboldened by our apparently insignificant
force, made a demonstration of attacking the guns,
and our position, for a short time, was very critical.
Not only was there a large force in front, but a
lot of skirmishers had very pluckily crept close to
us in the gram" (gram grows sometimes to the
height of ten or twelve feet), "and the bullets and
shot came in very smart. The body, who menaced
us in front, had got much less than 300 yards from
us, when luckily for us the infantry and 9-pounder
battery came up. Grape and round shot soon made
the enemy hesitate, and before the'rifles could begin
to tell, they moved off. Those on the right were
not idle, but owing to the broken nature of the
ground the charge was not very effective. Men

and horses fell in the nullahs, and two of our men were cut to pieces, from being dismounted. As soon as the enemy took decidedly to flight, Colonel Blake ordered me to remain and protect the baggage, which I did; and having luckily found my camels, was able to feed my horse. The pursuit was continued for seven miles, being finished at the banks of a deep river. Had the existence of the river in front only been known to the General, we could have driven the enemy pell-mell into it, and the slaughter would have been immense; as it was, I dare say 500 is about the number killed. We found four guns abandoned near the river. Tantia Topee was present, but made off with his elephants early in the day.

" Our loss (8th Hussars) was two killed and seven wounded; six horses wounded, and nine missing; the 17th Lancers had two or three wounded, and the Bombay Lancers lost two men."

When within a march of Seronge we received orders again to change our course, but nevertheless we *did* go there, for not only were nearly all the troop and artillery horses in need of shoes, but several of the officers' horses could not be ridden, as their feet were in so bad a state. The horses were also many of them without clothing, which proved very injurious during the intensely cold nights.

The monotony of our domestic life was at this time disturbed by the discovery that our Portuguese butler, hitherto deemed a respectable man, had been carrying on a system of gross extortion. We found that we could be supplied with the only procurable luxuries, bread and meat for ourselves, and grass and grain for our horses, at about 200 rupees a month less than the rate at which he had been charging us. European stores such as wine, brandy, beer, coffee, tea, sugar, cheese, bacon, &c., are only to be obtained at rare intervals from the Parsee merchants at Agra, Mhow, or Bombay; and as to potatoes, we have not seen any since we left Major Macpherson's hospitable roof in the Phool-Bagh at Gwalior.

On the 4th of November, the day on which we reach Seronge, with its tall and goodly trees and its fretted buildings, we heard officially that General Michel intended to return the larger part of the cavalry and the artillery to this brigade. Captain Heneage remains with his troop of Hussars, nor can we regret that an officer who has proved himself so energetic, yet so steady and cool when in action, and so efficient and popular when in camp, should have the advantage of seeing active service in the field. The remainder of the cavalry, under command of Acting Brigadier Colonel de Salis, were to have rejoined us on the 7th of November; but the Colonel sent word that they were so tired, and their horses in such an exhausted condition, that they were unable to proceed, adding, " *that a three weeks' halt*

*at least was required;*" but as his men and horses
cannot be more exhausted than the rest of the
brigade, I do not imagine that his reasons for a
three weeks' halt will be considered satisfactory.

Captain Buckle, in command of the Irregular
Horse, has given my husband some curious information respecting the habits of the Bheels, who have
made themselves so troublesome lately. They are
believers in witchcraft ; and there are persons
amongst them who obtain their livelihood by witch-
finding. A misfortune occurring to one of their
community, the witch-finder is sent for to discover
through whose evil agency the victim suffers. This
man artfully discovers some female who is the "pet
aversion" of his employer, and at once declares her
to have bewitched him ; upon which she is seized
and hung up by her heels. If the torture drives
her to confession, she is burnt without any further
ceremony. If, on the contrary, she persists in her
innocence, she is sure, soon after, mysteriously to
disappear.

We have been much interested lately by a history
of the Nana and his family, previous to the rebellion; and I venture to make a few extracts which
may throw some light on the apparently unprovoked
atrocities of this monster.

" Nana Sahib, Rajah of Bithoor, is the eldest son,
by adoption, of Badjee Rao, ex-Peishwa of the
Mahrattas. For many years previous to his death,

Badjee Rao had been a dethroned pensioner of the
East India Company. When in the fulness of his
power, he had, as a native prince, assisted the East
India Company in their war against Tippoo Saib,
the tiger of Seringapatam; and as a reward for
doing so, the Company, after years of strife with
him—after negotiations, exactions, and treaties, and
violations of these treaties on their parts—contrived
in 1817 to get hold of his dominions. After numerous and fierce conflicts, Badjee Rao, at the head of
8,000 men, with an advantageous post, was prepared to do battle for the sovereignty of the Deccan;
when Brigadier-General Sir John Malcolm, who
commanded the British force, sent a flag of truce to
him with proposals of surrender.

"The proposals on the part of Sir John Malcolm
were—that Badjee Rao, the Peishwa of the Mahrattas, should renounce his sovereignty altogether;
that he should come within twenty-four hours, with
his family, and a limited number of adherents and
attendants, into the British camp; that they should
be received with honour and respect; that he should
be located in the holy city of Benares, or some other
sacred place of Hindoostan; that he should have a
liberal pension from the East India Company for
himself *and his family;* that his old and attached
adherents should be provided for; and that the pension, which was to be settled upon himself *and his*
*family,* should not be less than eight lakhs of rupees,

that is, 80,000*l.* per annum.  After long deliberations
with his prime minister and other great officers of
state, the Peishwa accepted these proposals, went
with his family and adherents into the British camp,
and Bithoor was afterwards assigned him as a residence.  The East India Company, with their usual
grasping and illiberal spirit of covetousness, were
displeased with Sir John Malcolm for granting these
terms.  They could not recede from them; but they,
and the Governor-General, Lord Hardinge, took
care to limit the stipulated allowance to the smallest
sum mentioned in the treaty—namely, eight lakhs of
rupees, or 80,000*l.* per annum.  . . . .  In his
day, Badjee Rao, as chief of the powerful Mahratta
nation, had been a great sovereign.  He survived his
downfall—exercising civil and criminal jurisdiction
on a limited scale at Bithoor—thirty-five years.  On
the 28th January, 1851, he died.

"No sooner was his death made officially known,
than Lord Dalhousie tabled a minute at the Council
Board of Calcutta, ruling that the pension, expressly
guaranteed to the great Badjee Rao *and his family,
should be withdrawn.*  Nana Sahib, Badjee Rao's
widows, and the other members of his family were
naturally stricken with grief and terror.  They saw
themselves reduced to poverty.  They had no other
pecuniary support, than some trifling sum Badjee
Rao had left behind him.

" On the 24th June, 1851, Nana Sahib forwarded

a memorial to the Lieutenant-Governor of the North-Western Provinces of India, on the subject.    He was told the pension could not be continued; but that a certain tract of land would be his for life. The Commissioner of Bithoor, a man of high rank and standing, and who knew the circumstances and claims of the ex-Peishwa's family, forwarded an urgent and earnest appeal on their behalf; but in a letter from the Secretary of the Governor-General, dated September 24th, 1851, he received a severe reprimand for so doing.    His recommendation was stigmatized as ' *uncalled for and unwarrantable.*'

" After some further efforts, Nana Sahib addressed the Court of Directors at Leadenhall Street, in England.   His appeal was dated 29th December, 1852. . . . .   The Company appear to have considered that it added to their dignity to have the advocates of Eastern princes waiting in their ante-rooms. Somewhere about December, 1853, the Company sent back Nana Sahib's memorial to the Government of India, and the result was that nothing was done.    It would appear that Nana Sahib, with smooth and gentlemanly manners, unites superior abilities and passions of the strongest and most vindictive nature.    His spirit is high—his vehemence of the most determined character.    At the breaking out of the mutiny, which has rendered his name so infamous, he appears to have become a monomaniac on the subject of his wrongs."

Q

Three or four officers of the Indian army, to whom
I have applied for information on this subject, tell
me that the pension was *not* guaranteed to the
family of Badjee Rao ; but I gather from their
answers that there might have been some flaw in
the wording of the agreement which was taken advantage of by Lord Dalhousie.   Of course, nothing
can for a moment palliate the fiend-like atrocities of
this man ; but who, or what aroused the devil in his
breast ?

# CHAPTER XIV.

"I cannot rest from travel : I will drink
Life to the lees : all times I have enjoyed
Greatly; have suffered greatly; both with those
That loved me, and alone: on shore, and when
Thro' scudding drifts the rainy Hyades
Vext the dim sea."                    ULYSSES.

ON the 8th November we left our camping ground
at Deepna Kaira, where we had halted during two
pleasant days, and came to within six miles of Mongroulee, as Maun Sing was reported to have joined
a large body of bundealahs at Jacklown, and to be
meditating the plunder of the former place.

On the 9th we were rejoined by part of the cavalry,
and all the Horse Artillery which had been detached
with General Michel on the banks of the Betwa.
They returned none the better for long marches of
thirty miles, and sometimes more, a day. The state
of forty-four of the artillery horses brought vividly
before me reminiscences of the famous Danubian
reconnaissance. Their backs will not be able to
bear a saddle for many weeks to come. The Queen's
proclamation will, it is conjectured, cause many of
the Bengal sepoys to lay down their arms. Maun
Sing might also avail himself of it, as he has com-

Q 2

mitted no cruelties on the English, but, on the contrary, I am glad to say, protected and assisted several
ladies, fugitives from the Gwalior rebels, and forwarded them to places of security. It was well for
him that he declined to surrender on the terms offered
him in his interview with our Brigadier before Powree. They were, "Your life shall be spared, and
you shall have the same conditions which are granted
to the Rajah of ——."—" What are those conditions?"—" Oh! I believe they are not settled yet."
The Rajah of —— was made a state prisoner, and
sent to Sind for life; a punishment greater in the
eyes of a Hindoo than banishment to Siberia in the
eyes of a Russian.

We were returning from a ride, late in the evening
of Friday, 12th November, when, to our surprise,
we found the Brigadier had struck his tent. This
betokened a move, and we hastened to ascertain the
why and the whither? In consequence of some
information received about four o'clock, it was decided
to move instantly to a place called Dum-dum, where
Maun Sing, with a large force, was said to be
encamped. We started, not very hopefully, as we
had been cried " wolf" to so often before; but as the
day broke and deepened into sunrise, and then wore
on towards noon, the march became more and more
interesting. At half-past ten some spies, sent out by
the Assistant Quartermaster-General, met us, with
the news that Maun Sing's force had been that

morning at a village a short distance ahead of us; and on our reaching the place we found it plundered and deserted. Information was now eagerly proffered, and we found that the enemy were encamped on the opposite side of the river, distant from us about a mile. After halting for breakfast, under the grateful shade of some spreading trees, we resumed our route, and crossed the river, though not without delay and difficulty, as we had to find a fordable place as well as a pathway down its precipitous banks. Presently we saw, in the long beaten jungle grass, unmistakeable tracks of the enemy we were in search of. The trodden grass showed every turn they had taken. The scent might now be said to have been breast high; and it was followed with the eagerness of hounds. Some men running with all haste were speedily overtaken by four or five horsemen, who dashed after them at a gallop, regardless of holes, and stones, and hidden nullahs. They turned out to be Maun Sing's fishermen, and stated that the main body were about two cos (four miles) in front. The sight of a poor old man, with his arm slashed and bleeding from a sword cut, proved that we were still on the right track. At seven o'clock the Brigadier halted his men for a few hours' repose, which was absolutely necessary after being nearly *seventeen hours* on the line of march, during which only one man of the 95th had fallen out, and he was but lately discharged from hospital.

At the village where we rested, the monsters were said to have burnt a woman and two children about two hours before our arrival; and the inhabitants, who were eager for revenge, gave us, for once, truthful intelligence. The camp was pitched, and the troops allowed to sleep until half-past two: at half-past three A.M., without sound of trumpet or bugle, the men fell silently in, and we marched cautiously towards the spot at which Maun Sing was encamped. When we had proceeded about two miles the Quartermaster-General's spies again met us, and said that the whole camp was asleep, being perfectly unaware of our approach. I was riding with my husband amongst the advanced guard, and could therefore note how silently the men marched; the only noise was caused by a scabbard striking against a stirrup or a spur. Just at dawn the column halted, the 95th and 10th Native Infantry went to the front; the cavalry followed, in front of and alongside the guns; and a few minutes later the artillery broke into a gallop, unlimbered, and got into action at about 300 yards without a moment's loss of time. The enemy awoke, startled and confused. They turned and fled, leaving not only the whole of their camp equipage, but, in some cases, their very children behind. Clothes, food, arms, and burning embers strewed the ground, and several sepoy pouches and belts were lying about. We pursued at a gallop, the guns getting into action whenever an opportunity offered, but the execution

was chiefly done by the Hussars and Lancers.
Between 600 and 700 were computed to have been
slain; and the jungles were filled with wounded men.
Maun Sing, aroused by the first gun, threw himself
on his fast and famous cream-coloured horse, and
galloped for his life. His tents, camels, cooking
vessels, and clothing, all fell into our hands. Our
casualties were chiefly among the horses. Captain
Harris, Bombay Horse Artillery, was the only officer
wounded. He was shot through the arm from behind
a bush, in some jungle. There would, doubtless,
have been many more casualties, but the matchlock-
men had no time to light their matches; consequently,
the only shots were those fired from sepoy muskets.
Two Enfield rifles were picked up, marked Grena-
dier Company, 88th Regiment, and between fifty
and sixty prisoners were taken. We heard the next
day that Runjeet Sing, Maun Sing's uncle, was among
the slain.

Some circumstances that came under my notice
were very distressing. A man shot in the head, and
who was bleeding profusely from his wound, was
tended by his little daughter, apparently about twelve
years old, who held up her hands imploring mercy
and pity as we passed. Nor was I the only one who
tried to re-assure and comfort her. One of our
servants, when he joined us later in the day, brought
with him a little boy, about seven years old, whom
he found standing by his dead father, who had been

shot and had fallen from his horse. The dead man, the child and horse were in a group, and our servant charitably took the child and placing him before him on his own horse, brought him into camp. I became possessed too of a small white dog, which, together with a baby of six or seven months old, was found lying on a bed, from whence the mother, frenzied, I suppose, by terror, had fled, and *left her child behind!* The little one was sitting up and laughing, pleased at the horses and soldiers as they passed. This child was also brought on and given to the care of a woman in our camp, and the little dog was sent to me. I was told of a woman who, in the action of Beejapore, was endeavouring to escape with her child, but in the agony of fear she clasped it so closely to her side, that in her passionate efforts to save its life, she had squeezed it to death, and was still flying with it hanging over her arm, and pressed as closely as ever, but dead and cold. We halted for one day after the fight at Koondrye, where nine of the prisoners were shot before marching on the 16th towards Mongroulee, which we reached on the 18th. It seems to me that all this Indian warfare is unsatisfactory work, and although it may be true that in this rebellion severity is mercy, yet, on the other hand, there have been cases of ruthless slaughter, of which perhaps the less said the better.

We heard on the 16th that Tantia Topee had sent from the other side of the Nerbudda to know on what terms, under the Queen's Proclamation, he could give himself up. He was then making his way to Poona, near Bombay. It seems that his race, as well as that of Maun Sing, is nearly run, and with them will probably end all the disturbances south of Oude. A ridiculous report that Amba-Paniwallah, who is supposed to be at Serai with 4,000 men, has sent to challenge Brigadier Smith to single combat, has obtained circulation in our camp, and caused great excitement amongst the men. We remained three days at Mongroulee, as a halt was most urgently needed. Not only were there seventy horses of the troop of Horse Artillery unfit for work, but we were carrying about with us the men wounded in this action of Koondrye, and also Lieutenant Harding, dangerously wounded at Sindwaha. Persons who are not actually in the position of the sufferer little know what a man, weakened by pain, loss of blood, and want of sleep, endures—who, besides being exposed to all the unavoidable noises of the camp, is shaken up in a dooley for several hours every day.

The state of Lieutenant Harding was at this time most critical, as the wound, inflicted nearly a month before, began to bleed afresh. It was impossible to leave the sick in any place of safety, and as the brigade was so short of medical officers, it was equally impossible to send them away to cantonments at Saugor under medical escort.

Letters from Colonel Lockhart give information

of the rebels being at Bersea, not far from Bhilsa, but local intelligence reports them as much nearer. A body of men are said to be between Gurrah and Seronge, but I fancy they exist only in the imagination of the Nawab of Tonk, who is anxious for the presence of European troops near Seronge in order to assist him in getting in his revenue. A few bundealahs and others are still collected at Jacklown, but Maun Sing, after his flight from our brigade, immediately retired to Pardone, where he is living quietly in his own territory.

Tantia Topee has, after all, managed to elude his vigorous pursuer, General Michel, and also the troops and columns on the other side of the Nerbudda, and is reported to have doubled back towards the north. It is also said that he has detained the Rajah of Bandah a close prisoner in his camp, to prevent his surrendering himself* on the faith of the promised amnesty, as Madeo Sing and Beni-Madeo, two chiefs in Oude, have already done.

On the evening of the 24th of November, Lieutenant Harding died from the effects of his wound. The internal bleeding of an artery, injured by the bullet, could not be stopped without an operation, beneath which he must have sunk. He was reverently interred, beneath some wide-spreading trees, at our encampment of Deepna Kaira, nearly every officer of the Brigade being present at the funeral.

* He soon after surrendered.

When, on the day but one following, we left the place, the tree above him bore an admirably carved inscription to his memory, stating name, age, date, and cause of death.

On the 26th November, we moved on to Seronge, intending to halt for a few days, as so many repairs of tents, saddlery, gun-carriages, &c., were absolutely necessary. Colonel Scudamore, with a small field force, occupies our vacated ground at Mongroulee, in order to check any predatory incursions on that village. We rode over to see his camp, and in this land of wilderness and jungle, it seemed to us a positive blessing to see the fresh English faces of the 14th Light Dragoons and the 86th Regiment.

When we arrived at Seronge, a rumour reached us, through the medium of the dâk, that Brigadier Smith's column had come under the merciful consideration of the authorities. That the lengthened and unprecedented period during which it has been serving in the field, and the wear and tear of eleven months' unceasing work, on men, horses, and camp equipage, has induced the Commander-in-Chief to order the troops composing it to be relieved from active service, until such time as they shall be rendered thoroughly efficient by rest and reinforcements, or until it becomes again their turn to take the places of the relieving regiments in the field.

On the 10th of December, whilst the Brigade was halting at Beora, we heard that the Nana had crossed the Ganges, and, in company with Feroze Shah, was bearing down upon Bundelcund. Beora is a telegraphic station on the Great Trunk Road; and as we halted there for a week, Captain Shakespear, the political agent, who had lately accompanied the Brigade, was in constant and easy communication with Sir Robert Hamilton at Indore. We, therefore, received early intimation that the report wanted official confirmation. When it first reached us, it effectually scattered our visions of Neemuch, to which place we had a few days before received a telegraphic order from General Michel that three squadrons of the 8th Hussars should proceed, the fourth squadron going to Nusserabad. I sincerely hope it will not be our lot to be stationed at the latter place, of which an officer, writing a short time ago, says: " I trust it may never be your fate to be stationed here. It is, of all places, the most disagreeable. There is no drinkable water nearer than a mile, and no gardens or anything else to make life pleasant. We suffer torments from the mosquitoes, of which there are two sorts—one, a small lively kind, with curly legs, that flies about by day; the other, a large black fiend, which comes prowling out at night." Still it will be something to have " a local habitation," which is not taken to pieces and set up again every day.

It is certain that a body of rebels has escaped from Oude; and, in consequence, the Brigadier marched from Beora to Seronge, on the 12th December, in

order to cover Bhilsa and Bhopal. We arrived at
Seronge on the 16th, and soon after learnt that Sir
Robert Napier had been in pursuit of a party of rebels
from Gwalior, but had not succeeded in coming up
with them.

We now begin to understand the object of Tantia
Topee's erratic marches. He has evidently been endeavouring, by the rapidity of his transits from place
to place, to draw away or separate the British forces,
so that a passage might be left open for the Nana,
should he be able to escape from Oude, and desire to
make an attempt to raise his standard in the south
amongst the Mahrattas. The fate of Tantia appears to
be sealed: his gallant course must be nearly run;
and however we may abhor the crimes which he has
committed, we cannot refuse our respect to his good
generalship and brilliant talents. The chances are
that, finding all attempts at further resistance vain,
he will retire to some holy place, and, changing his
name and dress, will seek safety in obscurity. In
General Michel he met with an antagonist as indefatigable as himself. No march appeared too long
or too difficult for this division of our army: nor is it
out of place to observe that the portion of Smith's
Brigade which accompanied the Major-General across
the Betwa had, on its return, accomplished a distance
of more than 2,600 miles within twelve months.
And a squadron of the 8th Hussars, which is still
away far below Mhow, under the command of Major

Chetwode, has marched even a greater distance than
this.

We have just heard of the death of Brigadier-
General John Jacob, who expired, after a short illness, of fever, at Jacobabad, on the 6th of December.
He is universally regretted as a valuable officer and
an eminently practical man; and it is those who
knew him best who mourn for him most deeply.

The Queen's most merciful Proclamation, which
does credit to the head and heart of Lord Stanley, or
whoever dictated its gracious words, although it is
believed in and accepted by some, is received by
others with contemptuous incredulity or with open
defiance.

The *Bombay Standard* says—" The rebels in Bundelcund appear cursed with a disbelief of virtue in
human nature, and cannot conceive such a forgiving
spirit as our gracious Queen breathes in her amnesty
to her rebellious subjects.   Des Put, the leader here-
abouts (Srinuggur), on receiving the Proclamation,
deliberately put it into his pipe and smoked it, by
which he set fire to his own beard, as my respected
friend of the secret intelligence department observed.
But worse occurred at the village of Kool-pahar.
under the joint noses of the General, two civilians,
and a deputy.   Eight men-at-arms proceeded thither
to read her Majesty's Proclamation; the rebels slew
seven out of the eight, and the other they most fearfully wounded.   Such was the bloody answer these

monsters deigned to give; and these are Hindoos—
gentle Hindoos—the mild Hindoo with whose morals
Mr. Layard declares we have played the deuce."

As far as the last line goes, I, to a certain extent,
must agree with the gentleman whose name is quoted;
but the Englishmen in India are not all evil, if they
are not all good; and we must hope that the new
administration will encourage and strengthen all that
is good, and set its face against the evil.

On the afternoon of Monday the 20th of December,
some Lancers came into camp and reported that a
party consisting of sepoys with remount horses, stores,
spare camels, kit, &c., under command of Lieutenant
Stack, 1st Bombay Lancers, had been attacked by a
body of rebels, and that fifty camels and a considerable part of the kit had fallen into their hands. These
men were reported to number 2,000 or 3,000, and to
be encamped about twenty-five miles to the north-
west of us.

Brigadier Smith determined on starting immediately to punish them; and as soon as the camels,
which were grazing in the jungle, could be recalled,
the whole brigade moved, at eight P. M., to march all
night. How cold it was! Those who were mounted
found it impossible to keep themselves warm, and as
far as comfort was concerned, the infantry had much
the best of it. About six o'clock the following morning we halted at a village, and on making inquiries
as to the exact spot where we hoped to surprise the

enemy's camp, we learnt to our mortification that they had left on the previous Saturday evening, and were marching west! As they had two days' start and were all mounted, it was useless to attempt a pursuit, our infantry being already exhausted and footsore with a ten hours' march.

On our return to Seronge, we learnt that Captain Rice, at the head of a very small body of men, partly European and partly native, had succeeded in coming up with these same rebels from his camp at Arone, and had recaptured our looted camels, besides taking the enemy's camp equipage. Central India seems absolutely infested with fresh insurgent forces escaped from Oude. Whether the object is still to effect a junction with Tantia Topee, or not, we cannot at present tell; but we hear of rebels congregating on all sides of us. As General Michel is expected to move out from Mhow to Beora, we have sent out a party to Bhilsa. How much longer this desultory police warfare may be carried on, no one can at this moment conjecture. We returned to Seronge on the 23rd of December, but the brilliant weather and our unsettled movements destroyed all the peace and happiness of holy Christmas-tide.

From Bursad we continued our route, and after two long and fatiguing days we arrived at Chuppra. It was on the 1st of May, 1858, that we reached it for the first time, and on the 1st of January, 1859, about four o'clock in the evening, prostrated with

fatigue, we again sought a temporary shelter beneath
its walls.  Our march had been an unusually distressing one, as the Brigadier having received information that Feroze Shah was in the neighbourhood
with a large force, was anxious to lose no time.  The
worn-out baggage animals refused to answer to this
call upon their exhausted strength, consequently
those of the 10th Native Infantry were two days
behind, and for those two days the unfortunates of
that regiment went without food, performing on the
first day fourteen, and on the second day twenty-two
miles.  Fortunately we found Chuppra well supplied
and hospitable, but the news which greeted us was
little calculated to allow of halting.  Tantia Topee
had that morning been encamped only four cos
(eight miles) from Chuppra, and Colonel Somerset at
the head of a squadron of cavalry, four guns, and
180 Europeans mounted on camels, had come across
the rear guard of his army, without doing them
much damage.  This interruption had, however, the
effect of making the enemy hasten beyond our reach ;
and it was agreed at a council of war that the only
plan remaining for us was to hasten with all speed
towards Pooree, to which place they were supposed
to be doubling back.

The Brigadier, in consequence of a communication
from Sir R. Napier, changed his course; and in order
to strike into the Trunk Road at Budderwas, near
Sepree, marched the next morning on Shikarpoor,

R

and the following day reached Futtyghur. Here the clouds which had been gathering for some days came down upon us in copious showers of rain, accompanied by continuous thunder and lightning, effectually stopping our movements. So far as I was personally concerned I was not sorry, for the axle of our bullock gharry had broken ten miles on the other side of Chuppra, and the contents—my pet hare, dressing-case, little white dog, and sundry other valuables— were left on the road. Some invalid Hussars following in a cart recognised the little dog and brought it on; but I was greatly afraid lest the budmashes, or hangers-on of the rebel army, would find the wreck, and, after having looted the cart and walked off with the bullocks, would proceed to murder the driver. We were greatly indebted to the kindness of Captain Shakespear, who put himself in communication with the Resildar about it; and by his orders the cart was conveyed to Chuppra, and there left to be repaired. We sent one of our servants back on horseback to Chuppra to bring on the contents of the gharry in a native cart, and he did not catch us up for three days, causing us great anxiety as to what had befallen him; but he eventually appeared at Futtyghur, bringing the little hare uninjured, and the dressing-case, with its contents untouched. The same good luck did not attend one of my husband's brother officers, whose cart, containing all his stores—beer, wine, and a good deal of kit—none of which he will

ever see again—broke down on the other side of
Bursad. Another told me he believed his cart had
been going on the spokes of one wheel for a week, as
it had lost the felloes. Some things are irresistibly
funny, although bitterly vexatious.

On the evening of the 5th we were aroused from
sleep at eleven o'clock, and started soon after twelve.
We marched by an exceedingly rough and bad road,
over three or four rocky nullahs full of water, to
Kailwarra, and about three miles from that place
came upon horses' hoof-tracks, and several dead
bodies, affording unmistakeable evidence of the presence of budmashes. The information of the spies led
the Brigadier to believe that they were still actually
encamped at the village below us, and he formed up
his brigade in consequence, bringing infantry and
cavalry to the front, leaving the guns in reserve until
required. The hope, however, proved a fallacious
one; the enemy had left about an hour previously,
and were rapidly in flight. I believe they gained
information of our movements from the head man
at Naharghur, who had proved himself a suspicious
character before. As it was, we could not pursue
with infantry after so long a march, and the Brigadier determined on letting the men rest that day.
We accordingly pitched our camp, and on the next
day we tracked the enemy about sixteen miles
further. At the village where we halted several
horses were found, which had been left behind in

the hurry of flight; they were fine animals, but all excessively sore-backed, and in very low condition.

On the 8th the Brigadier learnt that Brigadier Showers was moving down from Agra to Jeypoor, which movement, if we progressed steadily in his rear, might cause Tantia to be headed back and so to fall into our hands. It would be a proud thing, if, after all, Tantia should be taken by this indefatigable brigade.

On the 9th and 10th we still followed the foot-prints, and on the latter day the brigade crossed the wide and deep ford of the River Chumbul. I watched a portion of the brigade crossing before me, in order to see which was the shallowest part, but as I saw several horses disappear in holes and deep water, and a gun carriage go in over the wheels, I very grate-fully accepted the offer of a seat on Captain Shake-spear's elephant, which carried over a party of five with great unconcern; causing, as he ploughed through the deep water with his enormous legs, almost as much noise as is made by the rush of water under the stern of a ship. At the village where we halted we were told that the enemy had on the pre-vious day but one looted all their camels, doubtless a valuable addition to their carriage. This part of Raj-pootana is a great camel-breeding country, especially among the Boondee hills, where we now are. On the 11th of January we were only about twenty miles from Kotah, and seventy-seven from Nusserabad;

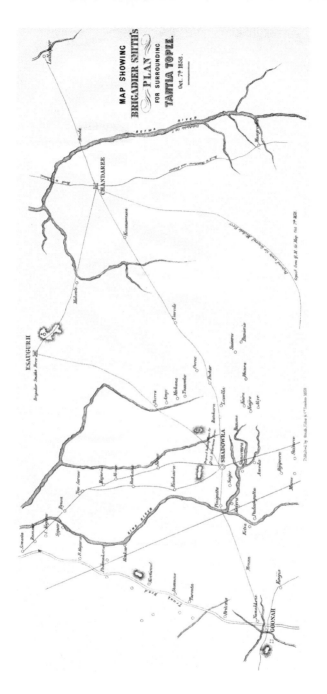

The material originally positioned here is too large for reproduction in this reissue. A PDF can be downloaded from the web address given on page iv of this book, by clicking on 'Resources Available'.

thus we have come round to the same point at which
we were this time last year. I imagine the Rajah
of Kotah knows better than to admit the rebel army
a second time inside his walls. The rich pastures of
Rajpootana contrast very pleasantly with the sterile
country we have left. The numerous and wealthy
villages are picturesquely situated, each on the
borders of a large tank, abounding with wild-fowl.
As we pass them before daylight they rise with a
noise resembling the whirr of machinery, and wheel
high in the air over our heads. Vast fields of wheat
stretch to the wide horizon, and give a cheerful
aspect to the plains.

A gang of thieves have been busy in our camp.
They robbed the Brigadier of his helmet, all over
feathers and gold, and then tried the tent of the
Quartermaster-General. He had a light burning,
and seeing the man's hand feeling under the wall
of his tent, made a thrust āt him with a sword, à la
Hamlet, but missed him. The thief then came to
our tent; but my small dog, sharp as a needle,
woke me when the man was within a foot of me,
and I could have cut off his hand with my Bhooj
dagger. He afterwards ripped open another part
of the wall of the tent with a knife, and took out a
portmanteau, containing my husband's office papers.
Disgusted at finding nothing of value, he scattered
them all about, and walked off with three bottles
of English ink. There were fifteen servants sleep-

ing round the tent, and a corporal and six men on guard at the time.

I must now, for the present at any rate, bid adieu to my readers; but I cannot conclude without expressing my gratitude to that good Providence which has brought us thus far safely, when so many have fallen round us, the victims either of accident or disease. Animated with this feeling, I close the record of our first year's Field Service in India, wherein that part of the Brigade, which was accompanied by my husband and myself, passed only one European station, Deesa, and marched in spite of Indian sun and Indian rain, and in the toilsome pursuit of an ever flying foe, a distance of 2,028 miles, more than 1,800 of which I have myself accomplished on horseback.

APPENDIX.

# APPENDIX.

ROUTE *of H. M.'s 8th K. R. I. Hussars from Mandavee,*
*in Cutch, to join the Rajpootana Field Force, and*
*thence under command of* BRIGADIER SMITH *in pursuit*
*of the rebels.*

| Date. | Name of Place. | Distance. | | Remarks. |
|---|---|---|---|---|
| | | M. | F. | |
| 1858. | Mandavee to | | | |
| Feb. 1 | Bara-Assumbia | 11 | 4 | |
| 2 | Maigpoor... ... | 12 | 7 | |
| 3 | Bhooj ... ... | 12 | 3 | Halted to procure full complement of horses. |
| 11 | Dhunnytee . ... | 16 | 4 | |
| 12 | Dodye ... ... | 14 | 0 | |
| 13 | Coombarree ... | 9 | 4 | |
| 14 | Chowbarree ... | 14 | 4 | |
| 15 | | | | Halted one day. |
| 16 | Jeesra ... ... | 13 | 3 | |
| 17 | Geree ... ... | 16 | 4 | |
| 18 | Moorania... ... | 12 | 3 | Between Moorania and Fowar we crossed the runn of Cutch. |
| 19 | Fowar ... ... | 15 | 4 | |
| 20 | | | | Halted one day. |
| 21 | Babra ... ... | 9 | 7 | |
| 22 | Warye ... ... | 13 | 2 | |
| 23 | Radhinpoor ... | 12 | 7 | |
| 24 | | | | Halted one day to change carriage. |
| 25 | Ooun ... ... | 13 | 1 | |
| 26 | Oundra ... ... | 15 | 4 | |
| 27 | Sommee ... ... | 12 | 7 | |
| 28 | Deesa ... ... | 13 | 5 | Halted four days for instructions. |

| Date. | Name of Place. | Distance. | | Remarks. |
|---|---|---|---|---|
| | | M. | F. | |
| Mar. 4 | Koachawarra ... | 16 | 4 | |
| 5 | Muddar ... ... | 10 | 6 | |
| 6 | Reodur ... ... | 12 | 0 | |
| 7 | Anadara ... ... | 10 | 1 | |
| 8 | Maira ... ... | 12 | 0 | |
| 9 | Serohee ... ... | 15 | 3 | |
| 10 | | | | Halted one day. |
| 11 | Palree ... ... | 10 | 2 | |
| 12 | Erinpoora ... | 13 | 1 | |
| 13 | Ballee ... ... | 18 | 0 | |
| 14 | Gomerao ... ... | 20 | 1 | |
| 15 | Sommair ... ... | 9 | 2 | Between Sommair and Jeelwarra we ascended the Chutterbhooj ghaut. |
| 16 | Jeelwarra ... | 11 | 0 | |
| 17 | Aimatti ... ... | 25 | 0 | |
| 18 | | | | Halted one day. |
| 19 | Lowa ... ... | 6 | 0 | |
| 20 | Gangapoor ... | 20 | 0 | |
| 21 | Gorlam ... ... | 15 | 2 | |
| 22 | Bheelwarra ... | 16 | 0 | |
| 23 | | | | Halted one day. |
| 24 | Mowa ... ... | 12 | 0 | |
| 25 | Shahpoora ... | 12 | 0 | |
| 26 | Jeetora ... ... | 13 | 0 | |
| 27 | Jehazpoor ... | 14 | 0 | |
| 28 | Thanna ... ... | 11 | 4 | |
| | Nonnegan ... | 8 | 2 | |
| 29 | Boondee ... ... | 10 | 4 | |
| | Jalnah ... ... | 10 | 6 | |
| | Kotah ... ... | 12 | 0 | Arrived before Kotah 1·30 A.M., on Tuesday, March 30. |
| Apr. 19 | Jugpoora ... ... | 10 | 0 | And remained in camp after the taking of Kotah until April 19. |
| 20 | Hunoutra ... | 8 | 2 | |
| 21 | Ahmedpoora ... | 12 | 0 | |
| 22 | Kyzabad ... ... | 10 | 0 | |
| 23 | Mukundra ... | 12 | 0 | |
| 24 | Bheeborra ... | 15 | 0 | |
| 25 | Jubra Pattun ... | 12 | 1 | |
| 26 | Usawarra ... ... | 16 | 0 | |
| 27 | | | | Halted one day. |
| 28 | Bunniagow ... | 14 | 0 | |
| 29 | Sathul ... ... | 10 | 0 | |
| 30 | Berodi ... ... | 18 | 0 | |

| Date. | Name of Place. | Distance. | | Remarks. |
|---|---|---|---|---|
| | | M. | F. | |
| May 1 | Chuppra ... ... | 10 | 0 | Halted to receive instructions from Sir H. Rose. The strength of the Brigade at this time amounted, including 74 officers, to 1,927 men. |
| 5 | Shikarpoor ... | 12 | 0 | |
| 6 | Narghur ... ... | | | Greater part of the Brigade made a forced march to Narghur. |
| 9 | Futtyghur ... | 15 | 0 | Where the whole force re-united. |
| 10 | Purwahi ... ... | 9 | 0 | |
| 11 | Jaighur ... ... | 5 | 0 | |
| 13 | Goonah ... ... | 13 | 0 | Halted for instructions. |
| 21 | Piniagutti ... | 12 | 0 | |
| 22 | Shahdowra ... | 13 | 0 | |
| 23 | Pulhar ... ... | 7 | 0 | Spelt in map Puchore. |
| 24 | Jharee ... ... | 12 | 0 | |
| 25 | Khorwassan ... | 3 | 0 | |
| 26 | Chandaree ... | 9 | 0 | A strongly fortified place, which was abandoned by the rebels on our approach. |
| June 1 | Mahouli ... ... | 10 | 0 | |
| 2 | Esaughur... ... | 16 | 0 | |
| 3 | Koosnaweir ... | 7 | 0 | |
| 4 | Pachouli ... ... | 15 | 0 | |
| 5 | Kollariss ... ... | 7 | 0 | |
| 6 | Sepree ... ... | 14 | 0 | Halted for four days. |
| 10 | Suttonwarra ... | 12 | 0 | |
| 11 | Chokeyra... ... | 12 | 4 | |
| 12 | Mahoni ... ... | 12 | 0 | |
| 13 | Arona ... ... | 10 | 0 | |
| 14 | | | | Halted to allow reinforcements from Jhansi to come up, under Colonels Orr and Hicks. |
| 15 | Antree ... ... | 9 | 0 | |
| 16 | Kotah-ke-Serai | 9 | 0 | |
| 17 | | | | Brigadier Smith's Brigade in action all day with Gwalior rebels. |
| 18 | | | | |
| 19 | | | | Brigadier Smith's Brigade in action all the afternoon, joined by Sir Hugh Rose. |
| 24 | | | | Shift ground nearer to Gwalior. |
| July 3 | Raliat ... ... | 12 | 0 | |
| 4 | Mohona ... ... | 7 | 0 | Where my little Hare was picked up. |

| Date. | Name of Place. | Distance. | Remarks. |
|---|---|---|---|
| | | M. F. | |
| July 5 | Chooselkaira ... | 11 0 | |
| 6 | Suttonwarra ... | 12 0 | |
| 7 | Sepree ... ... | 9 0 | The Brigade halted on account of the monsoon, till the roads became practicable, but on receipt of intelligence the greater part of the force moved out with great difficulty on Aug. 5. |
| Aug. 5 | Jheerie ... ... | 11 0 | |
| 6 | Powrie ... ... | 7 0 | Here they remained until joined by Sir R. Napier, and until the evacuation of the fort by Maun Sing. |
| Sept. 3 | Syssee ... ... | 6 0 | The whole Brigade marched to Syssee. |
| 15 | Lukwassa ... | 14 0 | Detained by rains. |
| 18 | Budderwas ... | 8 0 | |
| 19 | Meanah ... ... | 11 0 | |
| 21 | Goonah ... ... | 17 0 | Waited for orders. |
| 25 | Bhadore ... ... | 14 0 | Detained by heavy rains. |
| 29 | Amoda ... ... | 3 0 | Comet first visible. |
| 30 | Burkaira ... ... | 9 0 | |
| Oct. 1 | Goonah ... ... | 17 0 | |
| 2 | Punekaira ... | 12 0 | |
| 3 | Nya Serai ... | 12 0 | |
| 4 | Gatrouba ... ... | | |
| 5 | Esaughur ... | 14 0 | Halted to receive instructions from General Michel, and co-operate with him. The rebels abandoned Esaughur on our approach. |
| 10 | Mahouli ... ... | 16 0 | |
| 11 | Monone ... ... | 14 0 | |
| 12 | Serai ... ... | 12 0 | |
| 13 | | | Joined General Michel's force, and halted to try the possibility of crossing the ford, which proved too deep for infantry or baggage carts. |
| 14 | Rhait Ghaut ... | 14 0 | |
| 15 | Serai ... ... | 14 0 | |
| 16 | Narone ... ... | 8 0 | |
| 17 | Chandaree ... | 3 0 | |
| 18 | Pahranpore ... | 4 0 | |

| Date. | Name of Place. | Distance. | | Remarks. |
|---|---|---|---|---|
| | | M. | F. | |
| Oct. 23 | Serai ... ... | 16 | 0 | These forced marches of forty-six miles were performed by the Brigade, now formed principally of infantry. in forty-two hours. |
| | Mongroulee ... | 10 | 0 | |
| 24 | Bhorassa ... ... | 20 | 0 | |
| 30 | Malighur ... ... | 12 | 0 | |
| 31 | | | | |
| Nov. 1 | Moundlah ... | 7 | 0 | |
| 2 | Taal ... ... .... | 11 | 0 | |
| 4 | Seronge ... ... | 11 | 0 | |
| 5 | Deepna Kaira ... | 14 | 0 | |
| 6 | | | | |
| 7 | Bahadoorpoor ... | 11 | 0 | |
| 8 | | | | |
| 9 | Gadoulie ... ... | 4 | 0 | Were rejoined by cavalry detached away under General Michel. |
| 13 | Bukeira ... ... | 14 | 0 | |
| 14 | Rajhpoor ... ... | 9 | 0 | |
| 15 | Attakairia ... | 12 | 0 | |
| 16 | | | | |
| 17 | Tamasah ... ... | 10 | 0 | |
| 18 | Mongroulee ... | 10 | 0 | |
| 22 | Oudairah ... ... | 13 | 0 | |
| 23 | Deepna Kaira ... | 10 | 0 | Halted two days and buried Lieut. Harding. |
| 26 | Seronge ... ... | 15 | 0 | |
| Dec. 1 | Moondra ... ... | 17 | 0 | |
| 2 | Mucksudnugger | 17 | 0 | |
| 3 | Suttiria ... ... | 10 | 0 | |
| 4 | Beora ... ... | 15 | 0 | |
| 12 | Settewa ... ... | 14 | 0 | |
| 13 | Barode ... ... | 10 | 0 | |
| 14 | Sutherie ... ... | 11 | 0 | |
| 15 | Roosii ... ... | 10 | 0 | |
| 16 | Seronge ... ... | 10 | 0 | |
| 21 | Kalapoorah ... | 20 | 0 | |
| 22 | Kutchekaira ... | 5 | 0 | |
| 23 | Seronge ... ... | 14 | 0 | |
| 27 | Kutchekaira ... | 15 | 0 | |
| 28 | | 9 | 0 | |
| 29 | Bursad ... ... | 12 | 0 | |
| 31 | Bussawarra ... | 18 | 0 | |
| 1859. Jan. 1 | Chuppra ... ... | 24 | 0 | |

APPENDIX.

| Date. | Name of place. | Distance. | | Remarks. |
|---|---|---|---|---|
| | | M. | F. | |
| Jan. 2 | Shegarpoor ... | 10 | 0 | |
| 3 | Futtyghur ... | 15 | 0 | |
| 5 | Naharghur ... | 12 | 0 | |
| 6 | Kailwarra ... | 15 | 0 | |
| 7 | Relawur ... ... | 15 | 0 | |
| 8 | Mungrole... ... | 14 | 0 | |
| 9 | Etayah ... ... | 19 | 0 | |
| 10 | Kaira ... ... | 10 | 0 | |
| 11 | Inderghur ... | 14 | 0 | |
| 12 | Onearah ... ... | 15 | 0 | Making 2,028 miles since Feb. 1st, 1858. |

For EU product safety concerns, contact us at Calle de José Abascal, 56–1°, 28003 Madrid, Spain or eugpsr@cambridge.org.

 www.ingramcontent.com/pod-product-compliance
Ingram Content Group UK Ltd.
Pitfield, Milton Keynes, MK11 3LW, UK
UKHW010343140625
459647UK00010B/801